A TRUE STORY *as Told to*
FAY L. OVERLY

D1593417

ACCENT BOOKS
Denver, CO 80215

ACCENT BOOKS

A division of Accent Publications, Inc.
12100 W. Sixth Avenue
P.O. Box 15337
Denver, Colorado 80215

Copyright ©1985 Accent Publications, Inc.
Printed in the United States of America

Library of Congress Catalog Number 84-072590

ISBN 0-89636-151-9

Dedicated to
the police of Pennsylvania
and to
the community that cared.

"Oh that men would praise the Lord for his goodness, and for his wonderful works to the children of men!

For he satisfieth the longing soul, and filleth the hungry soul with goodness."

Psalm 107:8,9

MONDAY

MAY 4, 1981

Chapter One

Monday—May 4, 1981

"Will Ruth Fisher return to the stand?"

The demanding monotone pierced through Ruth's troubled thoughts like an arrow entering its unsuspecting prey. It couldn't be! Numbness overtook her. She hadn't expected to be called to the witness stand again! Shaking, she somehow managed to stand up and begin what seemed like an impossible walk to her sudden appointment.

Pursing her lips and fighting a feeling of weakness, she found herself facing the jurors once more—that sea of faces which she had analyzed and with which she had silently pleaded for three days. And then. . .there it was! Evie's sock dangled before her face! Instantly Ruth felt lightheaded; an involuntary sigh escaped from somewhere deep within her being.

The prosecutor, who had appeared to be sympathetic in the past, now seemed cruel in his flamboyant exposure of the tangible evidence. She heard herself explaining that this sock was one that her two daughters had worn interchangeably. But all she could see was the piece of cloth that had been stuffed down Evie's throat, cutting off her younger daughter's life breath forever. The navy and white striped sock was purplish-black from the collection of blood that had drained there as a result of her murderer's blows.

Ruth stiffened with apprehension as the manila envelopes were carried into her view. Somehow, with a strength that was not her own, she endured being shown photographs of their contents: Evie's bra, panties, top, and sneakers. Yes, yes, *yes*! They were *hers*! She fought back an almost uncontrollable urge to stand up, point to her former neighbor, and scream her accusation: "*He* did it! He cut them off her! Now make *him* tell exactly what he did to her. And *why*!"

Instead, she found herself faltering back down the aisle to her seat, crying silently as she passed the defendant, unable to bring herself even to look at him.

THURSDAY

JULY 31, 1980

Chapter Two
Thursday—July 31, 1980

Balancing the bags of groceries, Ruth almost slipped on a tiny blue sock, narrowly missing Evie and Davy on the floor. She sensed annoyance rising within her. Couldn't Evie have offered to carry in one of the bags—or at least have opened the door for her? Evie's preoccupation with her little brother, Davy, made her appear insensitive to anything or anyone else around her.

When Ruth and Davy had pulled into the driveway minutes before, Evie had dashed out of the house, demanding, "Where were you? What took you so long?"

Ruth had been indignant. She'd mumbled a short explanation, trying to cover her exasperation. Her daughter's recent adolescent impertinence and self-centeredness disturbed her more often than she cared to admit.

A sudden burst of laughter directed her attention to

Davy who was struggling to pull on one of his new socks. Unsuccessful, he tumbled backwards into Evie's arms. Embraced in a bear hug, he wriggled in a delighted effort to free himself.

Ruth felt a surge of guilt. Juggling a milk bottle and a pitcher of lemonade in the crowded refrigerator, she rebuked herself for her irritation. She should be grateful that Evie still delighted in tussling with her little brother. *Some* girls her age. . . .

Ruth sighed. She'd observed the masquerade that was characteristic of many young teens—an endeavor to hide their inexperience behind a mask of affected maturity. Evie, too, was struggling with changing emotions as she developed into a young woman. Only, Ruth wasn't ready to let go of her little girl.

Reaching into the grocery sack for the box of cereal, Ruth glanced at Evie. There were some who said that she looked older than her age. Perhaps. She was tall and slender and carried herself well.

Carefully placing the corn flakes on the shelf, Ruth had to admit that Evie's shyness and modesty could possibly be mistaken for the more reserved disposition of an older teen.

She smiled as she recalled how only a few hours earlier Evie had refused to leave her room while the upstairs bathroom carpet was being cleaned. Because a stranger was in their house, she wouldn't even open her door to permit her father and older brother, Terry, to carry the recently replaced living room carpet through her room to the attic. After much persuasion, she had finally opened the door a crack, somersaulted over her bed, and dodged out of sight on the other side. Andy and Terry had laughed. Evie hadn't considered it funny.

When Ruth turned from the pantry, she was pleasantly surprised to see Evie carefully placing the eggs in their individual niches in the refrigerator door.

She admired Evie's light, clear complexion as it contrasted with her long brown hair. She knew that Evie took great pains to keep her skin radiant.

"I can still picture you this morning when I went to your room, Evie. You looked hilarious with that Noxzema all over your face." Ruth's laughter rang out.

"Aw, Mom, it's not funny," Evie remonstrated. "I couldn't go to the bathroom to wash it off, even after that—that man had gone!"

"Well, I can't help it that we had to wait an hour before we could walk on the carpet." Ruth pretended indignation as she muffled a giggle.

"Dad must have thought me a weirdo when he saw me sneaking through the kitchen to wash it off downstairs," Evie continued, appearing not to notice her mother's amusement. "I felt like a fool."

"Oh, come on, now. Stop pouting. Your pretty face will be spoiled by all that frowning," Ruth teased.

Evie managed to smile as she walked over to the space Davy and his socks still occupied on the floor. Then her smile turned to laughter as she fondly picked up her mildly protesting brother. The mutual admiration that existed between them couldn't be hidden. Davy's "Emmie" was his favorite person; and he had been her chief delight since the day two years before when she had been allowed to carry him home from the hospital.

"Pick up the socks, you two. And, Evie, you'd better eat lunch before you go next door to clean Gary's house."

13

There was an unexpected gruffness in Ruth's voice.

"Must I, Mom? I'm not hungry, and besides," Evie added, looking at the clock, "I should get over there soon."

"Well, you have time for a sandwich and lemonade," Ruth insisted. "There's no hurry."

Why had her father said Evie could clean their former neighbor's house today? Ruth felt uneasy in a way she couldn't explain.

As if sensing her mother's doubts, Evie attempted to justify her afternoon job between bites of her bologna sandwich. "You know this is the last time I'll be going. And Gary won't be there. He's already moved. He called this morning from his apartment in Leola."

Ruth's uneasiness increased. She didn't like Evie going over there since Gary Newmen's wife had left him. She wondered what the neighbors might think. She had to protect Evie's reputation. However, since Evie's father, Andy, was home on vacation, she decided to leave the decision to him.

As he measured the living room floor for the new carpeting, he had called over his shoulder, "Everything seems OK today, hon. Mr. Newmen told her where the key would be and that she'd find the money on the mantel. Sure seems like he won't be around," he finished, as though reading Ruth's mind.

Glancing up, he added, "And, Ruth, this is the last time. There's nothing to worry about."

Ruth was reassured. After all, Gary had been their neighbor. It was just that Ruth felt he was different somehow, so somber, almost sinister. . . .She was uncomfortable around him. Ruth tried to shake off the

14

oppressive uneasiness. Andy didn't feel the same way about Mr. Newmen—so maybe she *was* letting her imagination run away with her.

Andy's appearance in the kitchen brought her back to the present. She watched him fondly rest his hand on Evie's shoulder as he complimented her appearance.

"How's my girl? My, you look pretty today."

Evie smiled.

"Where'd you get that top? Sure looks neat!"

The close relationship between father and daughter was apparent, and Ruth had to admit that there were times when she was jealous of that closeness. Once again her face flushed with guilt. She wondered if other mothers shared her frustration.

Checking the nails in his carpenter's apron, Andy left the kitchen as Evie gulped the last of her lemonade.

Andy was right. Evie *was* attractive. Her dark, luminous eyes were framed by matching curls, while her quiet smile accented them both.

A picture of Gary flashed through her mind. It wasn't possible, was it, that since his wife had left him he was attracted to Evie? Evie's older sister, Kathy, wasn't going along today. What if Gary were to come back to the house? Evie would be alone. Again, Ruth felt a foreboding about the entire project.

Evie's voice cut through Ruth's anxiety as she called, "I'm going now."

The screen door closed and Ruth watched her daughter walk across the lawn with a long, easy stride. Evie's unconcern was contagious. Again she chided herself for letting her imagination run wild. Neither Andy nor Evie was concerned. She was probably being silly.

15

Ruth relaxed.

*　　*　　*

Water splashed on Ruth's face as laughter rang in her ears. Abandoning her usual reserve, she reached into the wading pool and dunked a delighted Davy. His arms flailed wildly. The spray soaked Ruth's dress and, in spite of the heat, she felt momentarily cool and refreshed.

The cleaning could wait. Her mother's heart told her that these were precious moments which could never be recaptured. She had lost many such moments with her older children. She determined not to let this opportunity slip away.

The ensuing water battle brought a curious Andy outside to watch with an approving nod. Catching a glimpse of her husband's smile, Ruth allowed herself another boisterous round of merriment before leaving Davy to play with his toys.

Almost free from the tension that had engulfed her two hours before, she continued cleaning with renewed vigor.

She didn't notice that Kathy had come home from work until she heard a voice behind her.

"Hi, Mom. May I go over to Newmen's and talk to Evie?"

Nodding her permission and at the same time moving Davy's crib to vacuum behind it, Ruth again wondered why she had felt so uneasy.

Familiar daily routine, along with the satisfaction of completed chores, gave Ruth a sense of security. She began to anticipate her dinner date with Andy that night.

When Kathy reported that Evie hadn't responded to her knocking, Ruth felt only slight alarm. She was probably vacuuming, just like Ruth herself, she reasoned.

The afternoon passed quickly and Ruth began to hum as she turned her attention toward preparing supper for the rest of the family. She enjoyed cutting the carrots and celery onto the bed of lettuce. It was a break from the more physical work of the day. She was adding radishes for color when Kathy half ran into the kitchen.

"I just tried to call Evie—and she doesn't answer!" Ruth couldn't miss the urgency in her voice.

Glancing at the clock, Ruth noticed that it was 4:30. She frowned. It was taking Evie longer than Ruth had expected. She started to suggest an explanation, but the look on Kathy's face silenced her.

"Mom," Kathy began. She stopped. Avoiding Ruth's eyes, she confessed, "I didn't tell you before, but when I looked in one of the downstairs' windows around 2:30, I saw—I saw the sweeper—but not Evie."

Ruth's mind told her what her heart didn't want to accept. It couldn't have been the sweeper that had kept Evie from hearing Kathy earlier in the afternoon. Her previous fears returned with full force. For a moment she couldn't move. The knife fell out of her hand and clattered on the countertop.

"Mom, I know what you're thinking—Gary was so strange and all, but his car wasn't there, and it didn't look like anything was out of place." Kathy tried to ease her mother's anxiety.

At that moment Ruth heard her middle son's familiar footsteps on the porch. As Kathy rushed to open the door for him, Ruth thought wildly, "Maybe if he goes over, he'll find her—and everything will be all right again."

Ambling into the kitchen, Junior's natural smile faded as

17

he saw the worry in Kathy's eyes and heard his mother's command: "Junior, go over to Gary's house and tell Evie to come home."

Seeing the puzzled look on his face, Ruth became aware of the sharp edge her voice had suddenly acquired.

Mechanically rinsing a glass and finding a place in the cupboard for a misplaced bowl, Ruth's arms and legs felt rubbery. Carrying the salad to the refrigerator with trembling hands, she tried to convince herself that she was being foolish. When Junior came back, Evie would be with him.

But when Junior returned, he was alone. In disbelief Ruth heard him say, "She isn't there."

Before the full impact of his words hit her, he suggested, "I'll look upstairs. Maybe she's in her room."

Sudden hope renewed her strength. Running up the steps behind her son, she wondered why *she* hadn't thought of it.

"You're probably right, Junior! I'll bet Evie came home without us knowing it! She's probably asleep on her bed!"

Gasping for breath, she rested her hand on Junior's shoulder as he flung open his sister's door. Ruth's eyes searched every inch of the unusually tidy room. Evie wasn't there.

The realization that Evie was probably in trouble hit Ruth with frenzied force. Evie would not have run away, Ruth knew. She wasn't that kind of teenager.

She screamed for Andy. She could hear the shower running as she banged on the bathroom door, yelling, "Evie's not over at Newmen's—and she's not here! Hurry up! We've got to look for her!"

18

As she turned away from the bathroom door, a movement outside the window caught Ruth's eye. It looked like Gary's car. She clearly recalled Kathy's earlier words: ". . .his car wasn't there. . . ."

"Junior!" Ruth yelled at her son, "there's Newmen! Get in the car. See if you can catch him. Hurry!"

Junior ran out of the house and Ruth heard him gun the engine of his car in pursuit.

Not waiting for her husband, Ruth ran across their yard toward Newmen's house. Sobbing, a question tortured her mind, "What has he done to her?"

Reaching Newmen's house she ran from door to door, only to find them all locked as Kathy and Junior had said. As she stumbled in her haste, she saw Andy racing along behind her. Hysterical, she staggered toward him. "The doors are locked! I can't get in! What can we do?"

Without answering, Andy grimly tried to open several windows, but found that they, too, were locked.

Ruth moaned, "Oh, Lord, what will we do? What will we do?"

It was only when Andy found an unlocked cellar window that Ruth was able to control the overwhelming spiral of despair clutching at her senses. She watched with apprehension as Andy crawled into the silent house.

Tension mounted within her like a coil about to unwind, driving her to action. Looking in the kitchen window, she saw that the refrigerator was pulled out from the wall and the yellow curtains were thrown on the floor. Since Newmen was moving, she wasn't surprised to see that the refrigerator was away from the wall in order to clean behind it. But why were the curtains on the floor?

After what seemed like an eternity, Andy opened the

19

door, motioning her inside. Part of her wanted to dash past him and continue her frantic search, yet another part held back, fearing what she would find. Dread overtook her as she forced herself to cross the threshold.

Cautiously she opened each closet door. She was terrified to look inside. Would she find Evie tied up—or—dead? But an instinctive urgency to find her daughter prodded her on.

Finding nothing downstairs, she ran to the bottom of the steps leading to the second floor. The minutes dragged. Ruth could hear Andy's footsteps as he carefully checked each upstairs room. She hardly breathed. When he appeared at the head of the stairs, his face was ashen. One glance told her. Evie wasn't there.

As Andy stumbled down the steps, he said, "I'm going to call Mr. Newmen's parents and see if they know where he is. We've got to talk to him."

Standing in their own kitchen minutes later, Ruth watched Andy intently. Whatever Newmen's parents had said, it had hit Andy hard. After he hung up, he stood with his hand on the phone without speaking for a few seconds.

Ruth began to tremble as she waited.

When Andy spoke, his voice sounded strange and defeated. "Mr. Newmen doesn't have a phone in his new apartment. They're going to drive to Leola to talk with him."

Newmen had lied! He hadn't been talking to Evie from Leola this morning! They had been deceived! *Why* had he lied? He must have done something to Evie!

Anger and resentment threatened to explode within Ruth. "What has he done with her?" She was sure Newmen had kidnapped Evie. Her hands clutched vainly at the air, then fell in clenched fists at her sides. Fierce desire to do battle with her daughter's assailant surged within her. She craved revenge. Somewhere she had heard that she should love her enemies. But her natural instincts had control of her now. She was filled with hatred and bitterness.

Suddenly her body shook with sobs. She heard Andy dialing the phone and without asking she knew whom he was calling. She was glad. Finally they would get help.

Andy hung up the phone and patted Ruth's shoulder as he walked past her. In a few minutes he was back, holding Evie's purse and cedar chest in his hands. Through her tears Ruth saw ten dollars in each.

At the sound of a car door outside, Andy rushed to the kitchen window. "He's here!" he exclaimed, making no attempt to cover the relief in his voice.

Ruth stood and wiped her eyes as Andy opened the door for Officer Hartman of the New Holland police. Tears of relief rolled down her cheeks. Someone with experience was here to help them—someone who would find Evie.

Ruth soon discovered that she wasn't prepared for the studied composure of the law enforcement officer. She bristled under the quiet barrage of questions: Was there a possibility that Evie had just walked off? Had she gone away with a friend? Had she taken any money with her?

Ruth's patience was at low ebb. Forcing herself to control her voice, she hastily explained that Evie would have told them if she were going somewhere. In spite of her efforts to remain even-tempered, she found herself indignantly declaring, "Evie just isn't the type to run off! Why, she won't even go down the street to the park by herself. She has a fear of dogs. She's afraid one might run out at her!"

"Besides," she continued, her voice rising to a higher pitch, "if she were going somewhere, she'd take her purse with her. She took nothing when she went to clean, except a comb. Ten dollars are still in her purse and ten more are in her chest."

With sudden clarity, Ruth recollected, "And the money Newmen was going to pay her for cleaning his place was still on the mantel—five dollars. I saw it when we searched the house a little while ago."

"Wait a minute, Mom." Junior had walked into the room just in time to hear her last sentence. "When you sent me over to the house I climbed in through a basement window and saw $3.00 on the mantel. But you just said you saw $5.00. I'll go look again right now."

"Junior! Did. . ." Ruth began.

Knowing what his mother was going to ask, Junior called back over his shoulder as he shot out the door, "No. I didn't see Gary's car. If it was him, he turned off the main road."

Promising an immediate investigation, Officer Hartman followed Junior to Newmen's.

Watching him pull out of the driveway, Ruth repeated, "It's plain to me that Evie didn't run off!"

But was it clear to Officer Hartman?

*　　*　　*

During the next few hours, each family member tried to cope with the reality of Evie's disappearance. Friends and relatives vacillated between shock and sympathy. A heaviness attached itself to Ruth's heart and began to pull her entire being down with the weight of its burden.

Ruth and Andy had determined to stay up all night, waiting for some word concerning Evie, but as one hour meshed into another, fatigue forced them to bed for at least a brief rest.

Turning off the bedside lamp, Andy gently touched his wife's arm. "Let's pray for our Evie," he suggested in a quivering voice.

Ruth didn't respond. She had sent short, desperate pleas heavenward all night. They had been terse demands that Evie be found alive and well—and that she be found *soon*.

In the darkness, her eyes fell on the soft glow of the alarm clock. It was midnight. Turning toward Andy, she mused, "It seems like midnight in our lives, too. I'm afraid." Almost inaudibly, she added, "I wonder if God cares."

"Don't say that, Ruth," Andy quickly cautioned. He softly added, "The Lord will show us where she is—in His own time."

Hesitating a minute, he whispered to himself, "God has a purpose for all of this."

The words were faint but they entered Ruth's ears like a thunderbolt. "Purpose? Andy, what purpose? Our Evie is missing—*gone*! Who knows what that—that neighbor of ours did with her! And you say there's a purpose!"

"Ruth, the minute you came to the bathroom and told me that Evie wasn't at Mr. Newmen's, I knew that something was wrong. Right then I committed her to the Lord."

Turning on the lamp again, he held Ruth and looked into her eyes. "I *know* that God will show us where she is

23

in His own time."

Ruth detected hope in his voice. The steady gaze in his eyes and his strong jaw outwardly recorded an inner strength and determination that had their roots deep in his faith.

A moment before Ruth had vented her frustration and anger at God. Now further words of impatience and doubt remained unspoken while she studied her husband's face. She was supposed to have faith in God, too. Where was it? She wondered.

Andy's faith deserved a response. She felt compelled to say something that wouldn't shatter his trust nor betray the turmoil she felt inside. Half-heartedly she commented, "I guess we could claim the verse that says that all things work together for good for those who love God."

Andy squeezed her hand and whispered, "Amen."

He didn't know that in her heart his wife had added, "But not this, Lord. Not this."

As he turned out the light once more, Ruth stifled a sob.

MONDAY

AUGUST 4, 1980

CHRIST UNITED METHODIST CHURCH
4488 POPLAR AVENUE
MEMPHIS, TENNESSEE 38117

Chapter Three

Monday—August 4, 1980

Ruth lay still, listening to the songs of the first birds as they awakened to a hot and humid Monday morning. "Evie. Oh, Evie, where *are* you?" These now-familiar words unconsciously slipped from her lips. Staring at the ceiling which was faintly illuminated with the welcome light of dawn, she wondered, "Will they find you today?"

As she awakened fully, she was once again aware of the twin burden of frustration and despair which accompanied her every breath—threatening to tear her apart with their relentless ache. It had been four days since Evie had disappeared—and still no trace of her!

Slowly she sat up and gazed out the window at a soft pink cloud suspended against an azure curtain of space. Stumbling to the window, Ruth felt the soft morning breeze soothe her warm face and dry the tears.

Only last week, she reminisced, Evie had been bubbling with excitement over the remodeling of the bedroom her older sister, Kathy, and she shared. Ruth could still see her munching a cookie and declaring, "This is the only place I ever want to live. I never want to live any place else." Then just days ago at their mountain cabin she had confided, "I want to go home." A teenage girl desiring home! More tears rolled down Ruth's cheeks.

Another memory raced into her mind, the memory of words so painful that Ruth now caught her breath. Her heart beat wildly at the recollection. In an unexpected outburst of retaliation following a disagreement, Evie had saucily declared, "If I were missing, life would go on as usual in this family—arguing, eating, and sleeping!"

"If I were missing," Ruth repeated aloud. "Evie, whatever made you say *that*?" Annoyance followed on the heels of the pain. What had Evie meant—life would go on as usual? If she were here now—she'd see! Ruth's sigh turned into a moan. She couldn't stand the agony that was tearing her apart.

Ruth resisted the conclusion she was reaching almost unconsciously. Had Evie had some sort of premonition? Evie's two or three sleepless nights within the past month crowded into Ruth's memory. There had been no known worry or unusual excitement, yet in the middle of several July nights Evie had wailed "I can't sleep!" Once, at 2:00 a.m. Andy had read Scripture and prayed with her.

Desperately Ruth picked up her Bible and tugged at the silk marker she had placed in it the day before. She fought to concentrate as she read about the flight of the children of Israel from their bondage in Egypt and the ensuing pursuit of the Egyptians as they crossed the Red Sea.

Suddenly the words leaped off the page! "But the Israelites went through the sea on dry ground, with a wall of water on their right and on their left. That day the Lord saved Israel from the hands of the Egyptians."[1] If God could save the children of Israel, He could surely save one small child if He chose to do so!

A new strength and determination filled her as she entered the kitchen. It didn't last long, however. As she picked up some of the clutter from the night before, she couldn't escape the headline in the newspaper on the table: "WIDE SEARCH TO RESUME FOR GIRL 14." Pictures of Evie! Pictures of their home! Suddenly their lives were open to public scrutiny! Part of her wanted to suffer alone. But another part wanted to shout to all the world for help.

Pouring cereal into a bowl, Ruth reflected on the other children that the Lord had given to her and Andy. Each had their individual strengths. Each had their private temptations.

With a sigh, she spooned chocolate into a cup. Over the years she had alternated between feelings of pride and admissions of failure as the daily episodes of their lives unfolded. Terry, her oldest son; Junior; Kathy, and Davy were as dear to her heart as Evie was. How was this sudden change in their lives affecting them? Turning to the stove, she resolved to keep their private lives within the confines of her heart, no matter how public the search for Evie became, no matter how Evie's personal affairs unfolded under the scrutiny of detectives and reporters. She would protect them from the eyes of the curious like a mother hen does her young.

A slight smile crossed her face. "Well," she thought, "it

29

may be hard to keep Davy out of view. He just seems to be everywhere we are." Turning her musings into a prayer, she added, "Thank you for giving us Davy. What would we do without him to divert our attention from Evie's disappearance for just a little while?"

* * *

Ruth was still clearing the counter where she and Davy had eaten breakfast when Andy came into the kitchen.

"Hi, hon!" he said, his customary grin almost concealed by the determined look on his face.

"Where were you?" she asked curiously.

"Oh, I was walking along the railroad tracks trying to find some clues, or—," his voice faded away. There was no need to finish the sentence. Pouring a glass of lemonade, he continued, "I guess I'll go and join the searchers. There's talk of volunteers going out this afternoon to search around New Holland again."

"Just what *do* they know so far? Do they have *any* idea what happened to her?" Ruth asked in desperation.

"Well, the man who probably knows is in the psychiatric ward of St. Joseph Hospital in Lancaster. Mr. Newmen committed himself last Friday morning. But, as of Saturday night, police say they haven't talked with him yet. He has retained a Lancaster trial attorney as his lawyer."

"Why does he need a lawyer—unless he has committed a crime!" Ruth still refused to acknowledge what was beginning to appear inevitable. "If only they'd ask Gary what he did with her!"

A cup slipped from her shaking hands, spinning crazily on the counter where Andy grabbed it just before it careened over the edge. Heaving a sigh, she asked, "Where have they looked so far?"

"Saturday almost one hundred firemen and other volunteers from this area and Blue Ball scoured 2,500 acres of the Welsh Mountains on foot. Then, in the evening, search parties left the woods to comb the cornfields on Ranck Avenue. That's when I heard the state police sergeant, Harry Latsha, say that he keeps hoping to find her alive."

Wiping his eyes and trying to control his voice, Andy continued, "The police have questioned thirty-two people in our neighborhood so far and no one has any clue as to what happened. Donald Troupe, our police chief, says there's nothing else to do but search on foot—and keep searching.

"Ruth, so many people have come out to help look for Evie. And we don't even know most of them." His voice was unsteady as he shared, "A man told me today that he has a teenage daughter, and he would want help if she were missing."

Pulling a handkerchief from his pocket he continued, "Larry Usner, our fire chief, told me that the search for Evie is the largest in memory in this area."

Silence filled the ordinarily bustling kitchen. Each was deep in his own thoughts—in his own private world of suffering and anxiety.

Andy broke the silence. "Ruth, without the Lord Jesus Christ I couldn't get through this." He paused. "We must never forget that Evie is a Christian and—if she's not here now—we know where she is." With the strength of certainty, he added, "She's in Heaven."

Outwardly, Ruth nodded assent. But in her heart she wanted to cry out, "No, she can't be! She must be alive *here*, on earth—with us!"

31

In Heaven? A nagging question had begun to prey on her mind, to disquiet her spirit: "If Evie *is* in Heaven, then will *I* ever see her again?" Painfully, she had to admit to herself, "I'm not sure that I'm going there!"

Feeling Andy squeeze her trembling hand, she looked up, her eyes meeting his. She sensed that he was puzzled by her silence, yet she couldn't tell him about her feeling of helplessness and uncertainty right then. She was lonely and afraid—the same way she had felt three nights before at midnight. Only now she wasn't just afraid for Evie. She was afraid for herself, too.

Unknowingly emphasizing her agony, Andy held her and repeated, "Ruth, can't we thank the Lord for that blessed hope? We *know* we'll see her again someday!"

Ruth looked past Andy and stared at the wall. Again, she realized that she couldn't add to his burden by telling him about her apprehensions *now*. In fact, she wasn't sure that she could *ever* verbalize her fear. She must continue to talk of her faith in Christ. Maybe that would help to dispel the haunting doubt. She smiled ruefully to herself. Some might call her hypocritical. No matter. It would be her way of handling this spectre that had arisen to walk silently, hand-in-hand with the mystery of Evie's disappearance.

"Hon, are you all right?" Andy's concerned voice cut through the silence.

Almost mechanically, Ruth answered, "I just have a lot of things to sort out, Andy. A lot of things I don't understand."

He seemed to accept her explanation but was still insistent. "Ruth, let's have a time of prayer. It will help us— and others, too. We'll pray for the searchers. Over one hundred of them walked through the woods and cornfields yesterday, even though it was Sunday. Some looked for clues among the pipes, blocks, sand hills, and buildings at the concrete plant in back of Mr. Newmen's house. Some of the investigators have been working around-the-clock since Evie was reported missing last Thursday. We certainly should pray for each one of them."

But at the sound of the ringing phone, Andy jumped to answer it. When he had hung up he answered Ruth's inquisitive look, "Mr. Newmen called his landlord from the psychiatric ward at the hospital last night. He wanted to get some 'time fixes' about where he was on Thursday, but he didn't mention Evie."

Andy slowly shook his head. "Ruth, we need to pray more than ever before that Mr. Newmen will tell what happened to Evie. We must pray, too, for District Attorney Michael Ranck. I'm thankful for a man like him. He's been piecing everything together and admits that it doesn't fit the pattern of someone who just wandered off. Of course, we knew all along that our Evie wouldn't do anything like that, and now he does, too. And State Trooper John Ator also needs our prayers. With him in charge, we can be sure that the search is in good hands."

Two heads bowed. Two hearts prepared to petition God in the search for their beloved daughter. One heart was full of faith and trust. The other was filled with fear and trembling.

Almost as an afterthought, Andy raised his head and turned toward Ruth. "Everyone involved in the search is important, and I'm thankful for each of them—from the firemen, to the local police, to the state police, to every citizen volunteer. Who knows which one of them God will use to find Evie?"

With all her heart, Ruth wondered, "Who indeed—and *when*?"

FRIDAY

AUGUST 8, 1980

Chapter Four
Friday—August 8, 1980

Standing quietly in the doorway of her kitchen, Ruth watched Andy in the driveway as he talked to two men who had spent the morning searching nearby fields and wooded areas for a sign that Evie had been there. She sensed that he was listening carefully, appearing to question them every now and then. Shaking their heads, it seemed that the men were in agreement: they didn't know where to look anymore. The search had been extended to the Grace Mines area of Berks County near Morgantown.

"Maybe there—" Ruth sighed. Yesterday had marked one week since Evie's disappearance and they still had no hint of what might have happened to her!

Even Tracy Miller's Labrador retriever, Pepper, which had been brought in from western Pennsylvania, was unable to find any sign of Evie. For almost five hours Wednesday the dog and his handler had circled the borough water reservoir and other wooded areas, all with negative results.

By Wednesday, the number of volunteers had decreased to about fifty. Ruth couldn't blame them. The heat was oppressive and the outcome seemed hopeless. Ruth knew that Andy felt as grateful as she did to everyone who came to look for their daughter.

She had never before realized how friendly the people of New Holland and the surrounding areas were. Why did they choose to sacrifice their time and energy like this? Maybe one of the firemen, Calvin Burkhart, gave the reason when he said, "This is a small town. Stuff like this just doesn't happen here. At least, it's not supposed to."

But when and if it does, Ruth thought, they'll do all they can to help! And the police! Ruth never dreamed she'd be in the center of circumstances which demanded the full use of the county's criminal investigation force. Nor had she known just how caring and helpful they would be.

Investigators had tried a new tactic the day before as they had continued their search for clues. Two county detectives, joined by state and local police, had spent six hours stopping traffic at the intersection near the house Gary Newmen had rented on the corner of Jackson Street and Ranck Avenue. Ruth heard that almost three-quarters of the people questioned said they had passed by the same area last Thursday between noon and 6 p.m.

Had anyone seen Evie? She wondered.

Clenching her fists against the memory, she recalled recent reports of a foul odor in the nearby Briertown area.

The source had been discovered yesterday. It had turned out to be a bag full of dead chickens—somebody's garbage. The implication—the possibility—was almost more than she could bear. She found herself begging with every ounce of her being. "They can't find Evie that way! Please, no! I want her to be found alive! Dear God, please let her be *alive!*"

Oh, if only someone could talk to Gary! The police were honoring his attorney's request not to speak with him even though it appeared that Newmen was probably the last one to see Evie. This left so many questions unanswered. Answers only he could supply. Had he seen Evie arrive at the house? If he had spoken with her, what was her mood? Had she begun to clean? Did she give any clues as to where she was going? Had he taken her somewhere? He was acting so suspiciously now—guilty really, Ruth concluded in anger and frustration.

Suddenly she spoke aloud. "Why won't he talk? *Why not?*" At the sound of her own voice she realized that she was still standing in the doorway. Andy had moved toward the porch and she could hear him saying what he told nearly everyone these days: "I know that the Lord has a purpose in all this. We can't see what it is. But pray that the Lord Jesus will be glorified in it. And pray that Evie will be found soon."

Hearing a cry from Davy, Ruth turned away and looked into the living room where he was sitting in the midst of a collapsed tower of blocks. He had already begun to rebuild them, content within his world, oblivious to his mother's concern. Watching quietly, Ruth thought that their secure lives and family dreams had collapsed like Davy's tower. If only they could rebuild the pieces with the ease with which

Davy was working!

Suddenly feeling overcome with exhaustion, Ruth poured a cup of coffee and sat down propping her arms on the kitchen table. It seemed only minutes before Andy came in and joined her. He appeared more exuberant than her mood wanted to tolerate.

"Isn't it good to have friends who are willing to sacrifice their time and energy to help someone who is in need? I just shared with those two men what I told the newspaper reporters earlier this morning—how we're appealing to any person or persons who may know the whereabouts of Evie to please contact the police. I said, too, that we're asking everybody to keep praying for her return and to share in the glory of God."

Taking her hand, he softly suggested, "Ruth, I'm so thankful for these people, I feel like praying right now."

Without waiting for her response, he began: "Dear Lord Jesus, we thank you that you left Heaven's glory and came to earth to die on Calvary's cross. We thank you that your Word says, 'For whosoever shall call upon the name of the Lord shall be saved.'[1] We thank you that 'whosoever' means Ruth and me and our children. It means every volunteer searcher, every policeman, every lawyer; yes, and it means Mr. Newmen, too. We need your strength and direction. We can't go on by ourselves.

"Lord Jesus, we commit Evie to you. You know where she is. If she is still here on earth, we pray your hand of protection will be upon her. If she is with you, we thank you that she is enjoying your presence and the beauty of Heaven because there was a day here on earth when she accepted you as her personal Saviour."

Hesitating a moment, he added, "We ask that your

perfect will be done and that she be found in your time. In Jesus' name we pray, Amen."

Looking up through tear-moistened eyes, Andy saw a black form race past the window. His burden of the moment lightened. "There goes Dixie," he half-chuckled. "Someone is probably walking a dog along the street and she has to go investigate! She's getting pretty now but remember how mangy she looked when Evie first asked if she could keep her? She was a sight! I couldn't understand how she would want such an ugly dog!"

"But you couldn't say no, and she brought her home and cared for her like a baby. Evie wanted Dixie to grow up to protect her!" Ruth's voice caught as she continued, "Only I guess Dixie didn't grow up in time."

"Where was Dixie last Thursday afternoon anyway? She usually followed Evie everywhere. Why didn't she follow her to Mr. Newmen's that day?" Andy demanded.

"I guess she was tied." Ruth tried to control the accusation that was creeping into her voice. "Remember, you were going to lay the new carpet and you knew Dixie would manage to get into the house if she was loose."

"That's right. I tied her while I was working." Andy's voice dropped. "I wonder if she would have followed Evie if she had been loose. Maybe she'd have—"

"Well, there's no sense trying to guess what she might have done. All we can do now is find out what *he* did with Evie," Ruth said with a finality designed to cover her own helpless feelings.

"You're right, hon. I'll go see where they're searching today and try to be of some help. I think I did right in suggesting that Junior and Kathy go back to work. It doesn't look like there is much they can do here, except

41

worry. It will do them good to try to live as normal a life as possible. We must face the truth—we don't know how long this will go on before Evie is found."

Standing up and glancing uncertainly at Ruth he added, "I may have to go back to work myself before she's found."

As the screen door closed behind Andy, Ruth found herself unable to move from her chair. Staring into the empty coffee cup, she pondered Andy's prayer of a few minutes before. "*His* faith actually seems to be getting stronger! He knows that he'll see Evie again—even if it is in Heaven!"

Her thoughts wandered to the family's early evening devotions, when Andy would open the Bible for Scripture reading and prayer. Oftentimes visitors would be invited to join them, and Bibles were found throughout the house and passed around for all to use. Words of encouragement were gleaned from favorite verses as well as seldom read passages. Often a big smile would cross Andy's face as he'd exclaim, "Praise the Lord! Isn't that good! I must remember that promise!" or "I just know the Lord will answer prayer," or "That's great!"

Ruth sighed. Why couldn't *she* be as confident of the Lord's purpose and as ready to receive His comfort as Andy was? Unrest gnawed at her innermost being. She knew that she lacked the peace that Christians were supposed to possess. A feeling akin to panic threatened to overwhelm her as she realized that she had felt this same troubled spirit whenever the pastor had given the invitation to accept Jesus Christ as Saviour. Often she felt that she should raise her hand to indicate that she was a sinner in need of salvation. Why? Could it be that she wasn't sav—?

She stood up abruptly and tossed her head as if to throw the possibility that she wasn't saved out of her mind. Impatiently, she began to pull the ingredients for baking bread out of the cupboards. The flour canister and measuring cup banged on the counter. The shortening can teetered unsteadily, then crashed to the floor. The utensil drawer was slammed shut. Forcing herself to concentrate, the ingredients began to take form.

As she kneaded the dough, even her experienced hands ached. With every twist and turn the question pounded into her thoughts, "Am I saved? Am I really saved?"

Patting the dough into the dish where it would rise, a familiar Scripture verse, memorized as a young girl, flashed across her mind and into her heart: "Jesus said to them, I am the bread of life, he who comes to me shall not hunger, and he who believes in me shall never thirst."[2]

Standing motionless in the kitchen, Ruth whispered hoarsely to herself, "Do I believe?" Then, weeping, she cried aloud, "Am I saved?" Streaks of flour mixed with her tears. She determined that one day soon she would be able to answer that question.

TUESDAY

AUGUST 12, 1980

Chapter Five

Tuesday—August 12, 1980

As usual these days, Tuesday morning found Ruth tidying the house, trying to make it presentable for any visitors who might arrive during the day. Picking up several newspapers which had been left in the living room, she again glanced at the articles which described the search for Evie. The entire 2,800 acres in the borough watershed in the mountains had been extensively searched, and another 1,500 acres nearby had been covered. Yet, what seemed like an enormous area amounted to only a small segment of the mountains, only those areas easily accessible by foot and vehicle.

"So, if she's there, she could have been missed!" Ruth heard herself saying aloud. "But," she hesitated, "if she *is* there, she's—not—alive! Well, she's not there—she can't be!" Ruth's voice rose in an unsuccessful effort to convince herself.

Hearing his mother's voice, a curious Davy came running with outstretched arms, asking to be held. Rocking the wiggling boy, Ruth continued to read, finding that Chief Troupe now ranked the missing person investigation as the most intensive effort put forth since he had joined the borough police force eighteen years ago. With gratitude and wonder, she discovered that, like some other investigators on the case, Troupe had been putting in 16-hour days for more than a week. Hugging Davy to herself, she thought, "I'm so thankful they aren't giving up."

She looked into Davy's questioning face and admitted aloud, "Everytime I hear a state police helicopter overhead I wonder whether they have a new clue as to where Emmie is." Feeling her eyes moisten, she patted Davy and suggested that he play with his cars and trucks.

Staring out the living room window with sightless eyes, her thoughts continued to ramble. "I must try not to think about the state police scuba diving team in the borough reservoir yesterday, and the search with grappling hooks in the pond near Churchtown over the weekend. I can't bear to even hear the reports of the turkey buzzard sightings over cornfields and some of the wooded areas."

She was frightened—more frightened than she had ever been in her life. "Dear God—is she—is she dead?" Her thoughts had become audible on the last word. Now she whispered again, "Dead?" Pounding a fist into her open hand she cried, "No! I won't give up. I'll *never* give up hoping that she's alive!" But even her determination couldn't keep one question from entering her mind: *Where?*

As she walked aimlessly around the room, the words of

their pastor echoed in her thoughts: "We know that Evie's alive. She's either here or in Heaven," he had tried to reassure them.

Again, she heard Andy's words, "Evie's with the Lord."

Once more she could feel the almost unbearable inner turmoil. Neither the words of her pastor nor those of her husband gave her a trace of comfort. Why not? Was it because she, Ruth Fisher, wasn't sure that *she* was going to Heaven when *she* died? The tormenting question kept recurring.

Seeing no one in the driveway or yard—which was unusual these days—Ruth decided to go outside and sit alone on the back porch steps. Her heart throbbed and her hands felt sweaty. She *had* to know whether or not she was saved—whether or not she would go to Heaven when she died. Holding her head in her hands, she forced herself to remember everything she could about her earlier spiritual life.

It wasn't long until memories tumbled from the hidden recesses of her mind into a troubled consciousness. Forgotten feelings and questions emerged as she remembered asking her mom if she should put her hand up during an invitation when she was thirteen. She could still hear her mother whisper, "That's up to you." So she did. But she was still confused when she joined the church two years later. The minister had seemed to look through her when he asked, "Are you saved?"

Before she could answer, her mother said, "Yes, she's saved. I was at the meeting when she received Christ."

"If only she would have let me answer," Ruth thought now. "I would have said, 'I'm not sure.' "

Sighing and pushing a strand of hair from her face, Ruth

49

leaned back and watched two birds circling lazily in the cloudless sky. She hadn't continued to worry about her salvation, though. A fond memory etched a smile across her face. Andy had come along and they had fallen in love! The excitement of courtship momentarily erased the doubts that had previously been imprinted upon her mind.

Ruth strained to recall a special church service after they were married. She had gone forward during an invitation to receive Christ as her Saviour. Was she saved *that* night? Ruth heard the anguish in her voice as she answered her own question aloud. "Every time I do something wrong, I'm not sure! I just don't know if I'm saved or not!"

Glancing up in agitation, Ruth saw that the sun was overhead. It was past time to begin preparations for the family's lunch. She didn't have to do much cooking these days, though. The ladies' organization from their church, Love-in-Action, had been supplying one meal after another since Evie had disappeared. Their refrigerator was usually bulging with leftovers because their appetites weren't equal to the quantity of food being provided. Many times Ruth had to force herself to eat anything at all. Yet the gift of food spoke of warmth and caring more than words ever could.

Other friends and relatives showed their love by taking over kitchen chores and keeping an eye on Davy while Ruth rested or chatted with visitors. They, too, were a quiet source of strength, always there to lend a hand. Just as meaningful was their spirit of discernment that told them when their presence was no longer needed for the day. Ruth had been surprised to hear that some would not come to visit them because they didn't know what to say.

Dropping ice cubes into a huge pitcher of lemonade, she wished that others knew how much a sympathetic look, an embrace, a touch, a dish of fruit, a shared verse of Scripture, a short prayer, or just a few quiet moments together meant to Andy and her. As she tossed the salad, she agreed with Andy's observation: "Those who say the least mean the most."

Checking the casserole someone had sent for today's meal, Ruth realized that she was learning to *receive*. She had always found it easier to give, but now she had to learn to accept the expressions of love that were being offered by friends, relatives, acquaintances, and strangers. She had never had so many people come to her and tell her that they loved her—sometimes giving a kiss of sympathy and concern. It was overwhelming! Often, she wasn't sure how to react.

Slicing her freshly baked loaf of bread, she recalled Andy suggesting that her inability to accept kindnesses showed selfishness and pride.

"Ruth," he had reminded her, "God gave His Son, the Lord Jesus Christ, to take our place and to die on the cross of Calvary as our sin-bearer. In turn, we have to humbly confess our need and willingly accept His gift of salvation. Why, then, can't you accept what others do for you?"

She trembled with sudden insight as she took the strawberry jam from the refrigerator. "Is it possible—is this reluctance to receive hindering me from accepting God's gift of eternal life? Am I trying to *give* something, or *do* something, in order to earn a place in Heaven instead of trusting in Jesus alone?"

The sound of a car door closing in the driveway cut

51

across her thoughts, bringing them to an abrupt halt. Maybe there was news about Evie!

*　　*　　*

That evening, Ruth found herself in the midst of an impromptu women's prayer meeting in their living room.

"Goodness knows," she thought, "I need prayer. Another day with no word about Evie; I'm more unsure about my own salvation than ever; and every bone aches with fatigue. How I need strength to go on—not just physical, but spiritual strength, too."

A Scripture that had just been read still rang in her ears: "He gives strength to the weary, and to him who lacks might He increases power. Though youths grow weary and tired, and vigorous young men stumble badly, yet those who wait for the Lord will gain new strength. They will mount up with wings like eagles, They shall run and not get tired, They will walk and not become weary."[1]

As the ladies bowed their heads to pray, Ruth breathed a prayer heard by God alone, "Dear Lord, thank you for Jesus, the Bread of Life. I need His strengthening power in my faltering spirit right now. Help me to know without a doubt that I'll see Evie again some day—either here, or in Heaven with you. Amen."

WEDNESDAY
SEPTEMBER 3, 1980

Chapter Six

Wednesday—September 3, 1980

There! The last article! Ruth was exhausted. Clipping articles from newspapers and inserting them in the rapidly expanding red album had drained her emotionally. She was so engrossed that she didn't hear Andy as he entered the kitchen.

"Hi, hon!" Laying his hand gently on her shoulder he began to page through the album. "I'm glad you're taking the time to record each step in the search for Evie. So much has happened—" his voice broke.

Regaining his composure, he went on, "Remember how our hopes soared last month when the district attorney thought there might be a turning point in the investigation?"

"I looked for a miracle," Ruth added wistfully, "but it never came."

"I know. Our hopes were dashed when the police weren't able to proceed with an arrest, after all."

Not even trying to conceal his disappointment, he added, "The search was halted that day until the investigators uncovered some indication of Evie's whereabouts." Andy idly fingered the edges of the shiny pages as he continued, "And a few days later we were told they were seeking a search warrant to enter Mr. Newmen's apartment and car."

"Yes, here's the article," Ruth offered, moving the album closer. "It says that they will argue there is 'probable cause' that a crime was committed—and that the specific crime committed was interference by an outside party in the natural custody of the child by her parents, Mr. and Mrs. Andrew Fisher."

"The investigators used that little known statute because they can't prove exactly what happened to her. All any of us know is that *something* happened to prevent her from returning home." A tear rolled down Andy's cheek.

Ruth pounded her fist on the table. "Why? Why won't Gary tell what he knows?" This question had become a daily torment.

Paging through the album, she remarked, "Andy, here's the article that tells how Trooper Solt, Officer Hartman, and the district attorney went to hand deliver the search warrant to Gary in the psychiatric unit of St. Joseph Hospital. It was the first formal opportunity they had to question him about events surrounding Evie's disappearance. But—I still can't believe it—his attorney told him not to answer any questions!"

Ruth paused momentarily. When she continued, hysteria could be detected in her voice. "Now the investigation is stalled until they can analyze whatever possible evidence they seized during their search of his apartment and car. I just wonder what they found! Then again, I don't want to know. Lately all we hear are words like psychiatric ward, search warrant, possible crime, analysis of materials—" Her voice broke and she sobbed, "It doesn't sound as if we'll find her—alive. Does it?"

For several minutes the room was quiet except for a mother and father's heartbroken sobs. Finally, Andy began leafing through the album again. He read, "This, personally, I want to stick with until whatever it takes is done."

Ruth wiped her eyes and looked up. "Who said that, Andy?"

"Chief Troupe. I never stop praising the Lord for all the policemen and other investigators who are working on this case. We mustn't stop praying for them either. They need wisdom and direction that only God can give."

Andy continued "Listen to this. Four of our policemen have already spent close to 400 hours beyond their normal schedules working on Evie's case; and three state police investigators, who are paid by salary, have been putting in 12 to 18 hour days. I don't know how we'll ever thank them. It's such a comfort to know that they haven't given up."

"I never knew how dedicated they could be," Ruth agreed. "But then, I never paid more than passing interest in the search for missing persons. It never involved us before. . . ."

"It seems like they're willing to do anything to find her," Andy mused. "A team of scuba divers searched for her four weeks after she was first missing. They waded through waist-high water and foot-thick mud in isolated creeks and

57

lakes, picking likely spots where—where her—body—might be found." Unable to control himself, Andy put his head on his arms and gave full release to the emotion he had managed to partially control several minutes before.

"But they didn't find anything!" Now it was Ruth's turn to try to comfort her husband. "It was the second time they had brought the divers into the case and they didn't find—a body!" She wanted to shout that they wouldn't find a body, either. They would find Evie alive and well. But she couldn't.

Andy looked sadly at Ruth, ignoring the hint of hope in her voice. "Ruth, they—still—may." His voice faltered. "They're expanding the search to a 15 mile area around New Holland. The Liberty Fire Company has lined up twenty or twenty-five volunteers who work strictly with the police department.

"When I went along yesterday there were about thirty-five of us, ten on horseback. A lot were teenage firefighters who spent their last day of summer vacation on the hunt. We combed a 50 yard area on both sides of a five mile stretch of Gault Road. In some places we pushed through thickets and brambles where we couldn't see more than two feet in front of our faces. We stayed within shouting distance of each other and hoped not to meet up with any copperhead snakes."

Touching Ruth's arm, he added, "We can take courage in the words of Lt. Richards, 'However long it takes us, we're going to stay with it.' "

" 'However long it takes,' " she repeated flatly. Staring at a picture on the wall, Ruth intoned, "Today Evie would have been going to her new school at Twin Valley Bible Academy. She'd have been in ninth grade. Instead, she's been missing for thirty-three days! Be honest, do you think there's *any* chance that she's still alive?"

Andy looked sorrowfully into Ruth's eyes. "Ruth, I think we should face it. Evie is probably dead." Holding Ruth's hands, he added, "I can't see any way that she's alive here anymore."

Ruth couldn't answer. She felt empty and afraid.

"Ruth, don't despair. God is still on His throne. Just as we said in the prayer letters we sent out, we're trusting Him to fulfill His promise in I John 5:14,15. 'And this is the confidence which we have before Him, that, if we ask anything according to His will, He hears us. And if we know that He hears us in whatever we ask, we know that we have the requests which we have asked from Him.' "[1]

Ruth nodded silently as a lump welled up in her throat.

"Our first request in the prayer letter was that Evelyn—our Evie—be found," Andy reminded her. "Let's reaffirm that prayer right now, hon." Putting his arm around his trembling wife, Andy began, "Dear heavenly Father, we thank you that you know where Evie is tonight. We pray that you will soon lead someone to her—"

Ruth knew she had to face the reality that Evie was probably dead—and that none of her protests could bring her back!

"—and we pray that the person or persons who have taken Evie, and possibly harmed her, will confess. Give them no rest. Compel them to tell what they have done to her. We ask, too, that justice will be done—"

As Andy continued to pray for the police and investigators, many by name, a despair that was darker and deeper than any she'd ever felt descended on Ruth. "Help

59

me, dear God. Help me," she silently begged.

Then, she was aware of Andy's words, "Thank you for what you are going to do."

Somehow she forced herself to whisper, "Thank you."

WEDNESDAY

SEPTEMBER 10, 1980

Chapter Seven

Wednesday—September 10, 1980

"Oh Andy, come! Look! Katie and her children are here!" Ruth was putting the last dish in the cupboard after supper when she glanced out the window toward the garage. The outline of a horse and buggy could be seen in the deepening dusk.

Andy ran into the kitchen in time to see his nephew Sam tying the horse as his nieces, Anna and Sadie, clambered out of the buggy. "This is just what we need, Ruth!" he exclaimed as he rushed to open the door for his sister and her family.

Memories of fun and laughter flashed across Ruth's mind, temporarily dispelling the gloom which had settled over the Fisher household.

Andy's smile matched his sister's as he welcomed her inside. "How was the ride down over the mountain?" he teased.

Removing her shawl, Katie quipped, "Well, I didn't close my eyes and grab the side of the buggy tonight!"

Ruth remembered the icy night last winter when Katie's family had started across the mountain road to visit them. The horse's hooves had started to slide, leaving Katie shaken with the possibility of an upset carriage. Now her comical reference to this frightening experience caused Ruth to shake with exaggerated laughter. It was the first humor she had responded to in weeks and it momentarily flowed out of control.

Anna and Sadie stood shyly to one side, quietly enjoying the exchange of small talk among the adults. A hint of mischief gleamed in their eyes as Sam entered the door with a wide grin. "I really gave Mom a ride tonight! I didn't watch the speed limit at all!"

As peels of laughter resounded throughout the room once more, Ruth wondered whether people from other backgrounds realized how much fun the 'plain folk' had. Andy had grown up as part of an Amish family, and Ruth knew that he thoroughly enjoyed being with these relatives.

Katie's husband had died while he was deer hunting almost a year before, but she and her family were still living on their farm several miles away. Ruth marveled at her stoic acceptance of the events which had left the family fatherless. Hard work and endurance had always been an integral part of their life. Defeat was not in their vocabulary.

Still grinning, Andy led the way into the living room. There, an awkward silence contrasted with the good-natured banter of the preceding moments. Finally, clearing her throat, Katie asked in a hesitant voice, "What have you heard about Evie?"

Ruth's answer was muted by the familiar lump in her throat. Not much had been printed in the newspaper during the last week and there seemed to be a lull in the case. While she struggled to verbalize her thoughts, she heard Andy voice his concern, "Katie, I'm afraid the investigators have given up and tabled the case."

As his sister gasped in disbelief, Andy hurriedly added, "The police have tried to assure me that this isn't true. They tell me that they're piecing together the evidence they have. Meanwhile, they say, they're continuing to search for missing pieces in order to build a tight case. They won't name any suspect, though."

"Well, they don't have to!" Ruth interrupted in a futile effort to conceal the bitterness in her voice. "You yourself have said that Gary very likely has information about where she is. At the least, he probably saw her when she went to clean his house," she added drily with a toss of her head.

Andy nodded in quick agreement but continued defensively, "But I have faith in our law officers. I believe that they're doing the best they can under the circumstances. Mr. Newmen's attorney *still* won't let him talk, and that makes it hard—hard on the police and the district attorney—and hard on us!"

"Oh, Katie! I've told Andy that it seems like the midnight hour in our lives. Every waking moment seems dark and gloomy. I'm so afraid of what might have happened to Evie."

Ruth searched Katie's face, eager to unburden herself to one who listened so intently and sympathetically. "I just

65

know she didn't run away! You know Evie, too. You know she wouldn't do a thing like that. It's not her nature. She'd tell us if she were going somewhere. And she didn't take any money along. Now, tell me—would she run away and leave her purse at home?"

Torment was etched on Ruth's pale face as she leaned forward in her chair and half-whispered, "I lay awake at night with the fear that she might have been kidnapped and sold into white slavery! Someone said Gary had a lot of money that he flashed around that afternoon. I can visualize him tying her up—and selling her."

For a moment the tiny group seemed paralyzed by the thought. There were no words of comfort. Ruth buried her head in her hands and began to sob. Her voice was barely audible. "I—want her—alive—but—this would be so—horrible—I guess—it would be better—if she—were—dead!"

Lifting her head, she confided, "When I'm awake in the middle of the night I just pray. I pray that the Lord will keep a hedge around her, wherever she is. And—if she is at a place like that—I just pray that they won't be able to harm her."

Casting a glance at her own teenage daughters, Katie wiped her eyes and muffled a cry. Suddenly Ruth realized the shocking burden she had given to her sister-in-law. She had been so anxious to share the torment that haunted her day and night. Ruth wondered if it was fair to ask Katie to carry part of this heavy load—this weight of agony. Seeing the love and compassion in Katie's eyes, however, Ruth knew the answer. Katie would share the burden willingly.

Feeling compelled to go on, Ruth's words tumbled over

each other. "When I first knew that she wasn't at his house nor at home, I remember saying over and over, 'What has he done to her? What has he done to her?' " Pausing and plucking at the hem of her skirt with her fingers, she wailed, "I guess he killed her! But why? *Why?*"

Andy moved to comfort his distraught wife, but before he could reach her chair her mood changed from despair to anger. "Sold! Killed! Who knows what! And there he sits, in a hospital room saying nothing while searchers give their time and take all kinds of risks!" Obviously referring to their neighbor, she repeated with a hollow laugh. "He just sits there and refuses to talk!"

With increasing agitation she continued, "Remember the day I went along when we searched in the mountains? I kept thinking, here we are, tramping in the woods with the danger of snakes—and *somebody* knows where she is!"

Studying her hands for several seconds, she confessed, "Every time the phone rings, I jump, wondering if it's Evie calling from somewhere. I think, *maybe* she got loose." Brokenly, she added, "But—it's never her."

Entering the conversation quietly, Andy vented a fear of his own. "Sometimes, I don't really want to find her. Like the day we were searching the Welsh Mountains and we combed one area thoroughly because of the foul odor we smelled. I kept wondering, Is it—Evie? If so, the long search would be over. But it turned out to be a trash bag of fishheads!" he recounted with obvious relief.

Blocking the implication from her mind, Ruth hastened to continue her own experiences. "During the first days she was missing I thought we had a good chance of finding her alive. Two bloodhounds were brought to our house. I never saw dogs so *big*! The handlers were going to take them inside Gary's house to see if Evie had been there. The dogs first sniffed some of Evie's unwashed pajamas. But before they got to the house the men in charge were told that they couldn't use the dogs after all."

"Legal technicalities are so frustrating!" Andy interrupted. "They have to be so careful not to do anything that would cause the case to be dismissed, or to jeopardize it."

Deliberately ignoring the rationale, Ruth continued, "I was almost beside myself when they weren't allowed to use the dogs—not even to go into his car parked at his new apartment! Well—do you know what I did, Katie? I made a phone call and asked what would happen if *I* took the dogs over *myself* and allowed them to sniff around Gary's house. I was told that it wouldn't matter as long as I didn't try to go inside. So I called the handler and asked him to come back with his two dogs. He did—and we went."

Noting the surprise on her nieces' faces, Ruth smiled at her own uncharacteristically rash action. "The dogs sniffed and sniffed. The handler said it looked as if Evie had been in the driveway, up the steps, and on the porch. But we had to stop at the door!"

"See what I mean? The law seems to be on the side of the criminal, not the victim," Andy interjected emphatically. "For example, Mr. Newmen doesn't have to talk to the police officers. His attorney keeps advising him against it because 'he has rights.' But, I ask you, where are the victim's rights? Where are the rights of all the searchers out in the heat, pushing through cornfields, tramping through dense underbrush in the woods, diving in murky water—neglecting their work and their families to hunt for her?"

Katie shook her head in disbelief as she thought aloud, "So there's still no clue as to where she is or what has happened to her! After all this time!"

"Katie, I guess we'll tell you what we've kept to ourselves up to now," Andy confided. "We've put out a fleece. Gideon did it in Judges 6, and I feel that the Lord can show us where Evie is by that means if He wants to. Remember the story, Katie? Gideon was unsure that God wanted to use him in saving Israel, so he put a fleece of wool on the ground and asked that God make the ground dry around the fleece, but let dew collect on the fleece. This happened, but he still wasn't sure God wanted to use him, so he asked again for the reverse to be true—wet ground and dry fleece. And God answered his request a second time.

"I believe that God did it for Gideon, and He can do it for us, too."

Closing his eyes briefly, he continued, "Evie has always been afraid of storms so Ruth has prayed from the start that there won't be a thunderstorm where Evie is. We've watched storms circle around this area and wondered! Well, not long ago we asked God not to let it rain wherever she is. That way, when it rains, we can go and look for her. We can drive around until we find a dry spot and search it out. I even prayed that, wherever she is, that side of the road will be dry."

"We almost thought God had answered the other morning," Ruth continued. "Andy awoke early and said it was raining so he was going out to look for Evie. I told him that I wanted to go along! The roads were wet and we drove up Rt. 897 into the mountains. Then—there it was!

In a gully between two hills the road looked two-toned! One side looked wet, and the other side looked dry! Andy stopped the car to make sure. I held my breath as he stooped down to touch the part of the road that looked dry. I was disappointed when he said it felt damp. As we drove away we decided that they had resurfaced one side, giving it the two-toned appearance. But maybe we should check on it during the day sometime. . ." Ruth half-questioned.

Seeming not to hear her suggestion, Andy stated determinedly, "I know that the Lord is able to do it, but I don't know whether or not He'll be pleased to answer in that way." Almost to himself, he murmured, "I sure hope we don't miss His answer if He does."

"Katie, do you know what I told a friend last week?" Ruth continued in spite of some embarrassment. "I said that with all the prayers going up to God and our not getting any answers, I wonder if He's asleep! Of course I know in my heart that this isn't true. Andy keeps saying that He has a purpose in it all—and that in His time He'll show us where she is." Ruth tried not to sound as doubtful as she felt.

"Of course He will, Ruth. God isn't asleep. He is our Shepherd and we're His sheep. He knows us. He loves us. He loves Evie. We can trust Him. We *must* trust Him."

Andy's voice quivered as it rose with emotion. "God Himself will guide us." Finally, emotion overcame him.

Katie's voice was barely audible as she began to recite, " 'The Lord is my shepherd; I shall not want.' "[1] Her eyes were closed and tears rolled down her cheeks.

One by one the others in the room recited the twenty-third Psalm until Ruth concluded, " 'Surely goodness and

70

mercy shall follow me all the days of my life; and I will dwell in the house of the Lord for ever.' "

"Let's pray around the room," Andy suggested in his customary manner during devotions.

Ruth tried to concentrate on the petitions being sent heavenward. But the last part of the psalm she had recited kept going through her mind: "I will dwell in the house of the Lord for ever." Oh, how she wanted to be able to repeat it with certainty! But she couldn't.

TUESDAY

OCTOBER 7, 1980

Chapter Eight
Tuesday—October 7, 1980

Glancing at the calendar as she cleared the breakfast table, Ruth marveled that it was October 7 already. How could it be possible that all of August and September had passed with no trace of Evie! The dishes clattered in the hot, sudsy water as Ruth reflected on the latest news: a yellow trash bag buried somewhere in a Berks County landfill might contain the remains of Ev—.

"No!" she cried. A glass slipped off the counter and broke into a hundred pieces. Shattered—like her hopes.

Stooping to brush the pieces into a dustpan, she heard a rap at the kitchen door. Before she could answer, her close friend, Melinda, came in with a friendly, "Hi! How are you this morning?"

Seeing that there were still dishes in the sink, Melinda put on an apron and finished washing them as Ruth tidied the dining area.

"I'm glad you came, Melinda," Ruth confided. "I need someone to listen to me today! I was just thinking about the search at the landfill. If that yellow bag the trash men picked up at the cemetery smelled so bad, why didn't they check it out right away? Now the investigators are depending on dogs! Did you know that they think human remains have been in the barrel?"

Picking up a towel to dry the dishes, she added in a hollow voice, "And the police think it may have been Evie."

She stood holding a plate in her hand, transfixed by the horrible scene in her mind. Then her voice rose. "Berks Landfill! It's just a dump—a dump, mind you! And they're looking for *my girl* there! They've dug through ten million pounds of garbage for four weeks looking for my Evie!"

Drying dishes at a furious pace, Ruth almost screamed, "They still say they can't prove that a crime has been committed! No *crime*—even though the district attorney said at the end of September that they suspect Evie's body is buried somewhere beneath tons of garbage!"

Giving Melinda an imploring look, her voice caught as she continued, "Now there's talk of stopping the search at the landfill. What then?"

Melinda's troubled eyes reflected Ruth's as she suggested, "There's always the man in the psychiatric ward who could probably tell them just where to look for Evie, or at least whether he was the last one to see her."

Before Ruth could respond, Melinda offered to take her along on a search of their own.

"Oh, Melinda, remember the other week when we helped search, I was afraid to look—and afraid not to look!

I was afraid I'd find something, and afraid I wouldn't find anything! I guess that's why they don't want Andy or me to help with the landfill search. If they'd find Evie while we're there—in that condition—I'm not sure how I'd take it!"

Tension filled the kitchen as Ruth deliberately removed her apron and folded it with exaggerated neatness. Her voice was carefully controlled as she decided, "No, from now on I'll leave the searching to others."

Melinda's eyes were wet as she gave Ruth an understanding hug before hurrying to her car.

A few minutes later, when Ruth came down the stairs with the clothes hamper, she heard Andy enter the kitchen. As she sorted the wash in the laundry room, he explained the concerned look on his face.

"I went to see Mr. Newmen today at St. Joe's Hospital."

The words hit Ruth like an explosion. "You what?" she exclaimed, dropping the towels into the washer.

"I've been thinking about it for a long time and this morning I made up my mind to do it. I've been wanting to talk to him myself."

"Well? What did he say? Tell me," Ruth demanded.

"When I got there, I was told that he had just been transferred to Harrisburg State Hospital."

"Transferred! Why? When did they decide to do that?" she shrieked.

Andy only shrugged his shoulders, his head lowered.

Ruth walked into the kitchen and Andy watched as she poured lemonade before joining him at the table. He confided quietly, "Ruth, I feel that something has to happen soon. The searchers have done a tremendous job so far. The number of volunteers at the landfill increased from a dozen to about seventy-five the middle of September. But by the beginning of this month, there were only twenty, and today there were fewer than ten. I feel that we've disappointed a lot of them by not allowing the psychics to come into the case. Some feel that we're neglecting an important source of information."

"But we don't believe that psychics are of God. We believe they receive their powers from Satan. I agree with you, Andy. Let's wait and let God do it in His time and according to His purpose. We want God to get the glory for finding Evie when—and if—she's found."

"Now, Ruth," Andy chided, "I just detected doubt. Don't say, 'if.' He *is* able. He is not limited." Taking her hands in his, he reminded her, "Ruth, never forget, God *is* going to have His way in this. We're given only one part at a time, not the whole picture. We must trust Him. He won't fail us."

*   *   *

That evening as Andy moved his finger down the verses in Ephesians 6, one of them seemed to stand out from the rest: "Put on the full armor of God, that you may be able to stand firm against the schemes of the devil."[1]

The Fishers had received numerous phone calls urging them to allow the police to use psychics. In fact, several times Andy was suspicious that they *were* consulted by some of the investigators without his permission.

"Ruth, I certainly don't want to interfere with the investigation, but this verse explains why I requested that no psychics be called in. I believe that they are part of the devil's schemes. I have a right to my opinion and beliefs, don't I?"

"Andy, what would you do if they went ahead and

consulted one anyway?" Ruth questioned.

Hesitating, he responded, "Well, I guess I wouldn't jump all over the police if a psychic does, somehow, become involved. After all, the law does have the authority over us."

Thrusting the Bible into Ruth's hands, he requested her to read on.

" 'For our struggle is not against flesh and blood, but against the rulers, against the powers, against the world forces of this darkness, against the spiritual forces of wickedness in the heavenly places.'[2]

"Andy, this reminds me of the verses in Exodus 7 that you quoted to the newspaper reporters—where Aaron cast down his rod before pharaoh and the rod became a serpent. When pharaoh called his wise men and sorcerers to repeat the miracle, they did, but then Aaron's rod swallowed up their rods."

"Yes, I believe that mentalists are like the pharaoh's soothsayers. They have the power to accomplish certain miracles, but they're always overpowered by God."

Ruth's humorless laugh seemed to startle Andy, but she began to speak before he could question her. "I just thought of the dowser from Chester County who brought his divining stick to the landfill and left two hours later, convinced that he had found the spot where Evie was buried.

"I heard one trooper say he'd like to believe him, but as a policeman he had to have evidence and the dowser's assertion defied logic. I don't think they appreciated his 'finding.' "

Incredulously, Andy recalled, "Here again, some people believed that he and his forked twig had actually found the location of Evie's body."

Ruth shuddered as the words, "Evie's body," hammered their way into her innermost being. She was still trembling as Andy took the Bible from her and continued reading. " 'In addition to all this, take up the shield of faith with which you will be able to extinguish all the flaming missiles of the evil one. And take the helmet of salvation and the sword of the Spirit, which is the Word of God. With all prayer. . . .'[3]

"Ruth, here's the answer to our dilemma! Our faith needs to be coupled with the Word and prayer. That's the key to victory! Even if the whole world turns against us, since we know that what we are doing is right, we have to do it! We dare not try to please men. We must try to please God."

"Please *God*?!" Ruth's thoughts broke off and abruptly stopped at the ringing of the telephone.

WEDNESDAY

OCTOBER 8, 1980

Chapter Nine
Wednesday—October 8, 1980

"Be with you in a minute, hon!" Andy folded the dough one more time before he finished kneading his fourth loaf of bread. Pushing a pan aside, he arranged his creations on the counter next to the dishes which had been left to dry after supper.

Ruth looked up as she turned a page of the evening paper. Lines of weariness were etched on Andy's face. His day had begun at 3:00 a.m. at the bakery. Although he enjoyed his work, she knew that the landfill search, which had entered the fifth week, was never far from his mind. Only nine volunteers had shown up today. Their unpleasant task had been fruitless. They had processed fifty-two truckloads of garbage without any trace of Evie.

Finally, pulling his chair next to Ruth, Andy frowned. "Something puzzles me, Ruth. The police are looking for a ten foot length of quarter-inch rope and a blanket or quilt, red or pink in color. I know they'd give away their investigation if they told all they know, but it makes me curious."

"We got a phone call today that revealed more news, too," Ruth said with an edge of sarcasm to her voice. "Someone reported that Gary was arrested in 1970 for assaulting an Amish girl along a West Earl Township road. At first he had pleaded 'not guilty,' but at the trial he changed his plea to 'guilty.' At that time he was fined $25, ordered to pay court costs and put on one year probation."

"Yes, someone told me about it at work. A reporter dug that up, I heard." Andy tried unsuccessfully to control the anger that was creeping into his voice. "I just didn't want to mention—or think about it—until after supper. From what I've heard, if her father hadn't seen him grabbing her, it might have been another Evie case."

Ruth wanted to scream, "Andy, don't say that! Do you know what that implies! Evie—assaulted—and then—"

But before she could verbalize her fear, Dixie barked and Ruth heard a rap on the kitchen door. The distraction was a welcome relief, and she managed a smile at their friends, Tom and Sue Taylor, who were standing at the door. Little Davy seemed to sense the presence of other small children, for he came running from nowhere to greet Andy and Kim who had come along. After guiding the children to the toy chest, the grown-ups settled down for a cup of coffee and a time of sharing.

"You know, Tom, you'd have been Evie's principal if she were here. She'd have been one of your ninth grade pupils at the academy." The pain in Andy's voice almost erased the feeling of well-being that had arisen at the appearance of their visitors.

Summoning all the courage she could muster, Ruth interjected, "Maybe she'll be there yet. I hope you still have room for her." In an effort to confirm the possibility, Ruth's moist eyes searched Tom's face for a favorable reaction.

Tom cleared his throat before he quietly commented, "Yes, I'm sure we'd find a place for her." Hesitating a moment, he continued in a more fervent tone, "You know the entire school is praying that Evie will be found soon. Even those as young as second grade have a special prayer time for her each morning."

Continuing in the positive manner begun by her husband, Sue inquired, "Did I hear that you had the opportunity to lead one of the searchers to the Lord? Someone was telling me about a young man by the name of Howard."

Now Andy grinned. "Oh, yes. It's just precious. He lives in Lancaster and came out to search for Evie. We didn't know Howard before, but he came to the house one evening and, while we were chatting, I found out that he wasn't saved. I told him that he could be as certain as Evie had been that he would go to Heaven when he died.

"We opened a Bible and I showed him the plan of salvation. I explained how Jesus offered Himself as a sacrifice on the cross of Calvary for our sins, and told him about the promises of God. Then we prayed together. He admitted that he was a sinner and needed a Saviour. He believed that Jesus died on the cross in his place, and he asked Jesus to save him. It was so neat to assure him that, according to God's Word, he has everlasting life."

"Amen," agreed Tom. "It's sad that there are many today who feel they can't know until some future judgment day whether or not they are saved."

All the time Ruth had listened quietly. Mentally, she knew that all they were saying was true. Again, she wondered if she had ever sincerely admitted that she was a sinner and called upon the Lord to save her. Something inside said, "Well, make sure now." But pride pulled the other way and cautioned, "What will the Taylors think?"

Turning her troubled thoughts back to her guests, she heard Tom saying to Andy, "I've heard that you're from an Amish background, but I've never heard your testimony. Since the Lord has given you the opportunity to witness to others, I'm wondering how you, yourself, were saved."

"Oh, I'll be glad to tell you," Andy eagerly replied. "It's true that I was raised Amish, but I guess their different customs kept me from joining." He seemed deep in thought for a long moment of silence.

Ruth watched his eyes as they fixed on his empty coffee cup before he simply said, "Instead, I joined the United Brethren Church."

Ruth knew that he had deliberately chosen to block the disturbing memories from his mind. She hoped their friends would understand his unexplained reluctance to share details of his life with the Amish. Looking up, he continued, "At that time, I remember the preacher asking, 'Do you believe that the Lord Jesus Christ is the Son of God, and do you accept Him as your personal Saviour?' "

Glancing at Ruth, Andy went on. "I said, 'I do,' and I really believe that I did. But I didn't have the assurance of my salvation."

Ruth stifled a sob. She had a sudden urge to leave the room. Maybe she could excuse herself to check on the children. Or to make sure that the dogs were tied. Anything so as not to have to face her uncertainty *again* through Andy's testimony.

Instead, she shifted her position, sitting stiffly in her chair. Silently she scolded herself for not being mature enough to face her problems without nursing a childish desire to run away from them. She forced herself to listen as Andy continued.

"Many times after that when I'd go to evangelistic meetings I wanted to go to the altar. Then I'd think, 'Why do you want to do that? You're already saved.' But when I'd feel like witnessing to someone, I'd think, 'Why do you want to witness? You're not even sure *you're* saved.'

"It wasn't long until I joined the military and was given a Gideon Bible and a New Testament. I remember sitting in a tent one day in Korea. I turned to the back page of the New Testament where the sinner's prayer of repentance was printed and I read it carefully. Then I prayed something to this effect, 'Lord, I really want to be saved. I'm not sure I am.'

"One night after I was home and after Ruth and I were married, we went to a Youth for Christ meeting in Lancaster. There was an invitation for those who thought they were saved, but weren't sure. We were asked to raise our hands, and, of course, I did." He chuckled to himself, seemingly oblivious to his listeners.

"Bob Neff was pointing out hands all over McCaskey Auditorium, and then he pointed in my direction. He said that he had seen one hand underneath the balcony. I knew it had been mine!" Andy paused, engrossed in his memories. "I decided to go forward, and in the counseling room I received assurance of my salvation. I can truthfully say from that night to this I have never again doubted that

87

I'm saved."

"How did the counselor assure you, finally?" Tom gently prodded.

"A personal worker explained that you're saved by simply believing what God has said. You don't look for feelings. You just believe exactly what God has said," he reiterated.

Ruth was glad no one seemed to notice her discomfort. She did believe—or didn't she? She was about to get up and prepare refreshments when Andy went on. Something about his serious demeanor made her postpone getting the cake and ice cream.

Looking at his folded hands, Andy admitted, "My Christian life hasn't experienced a fast growth. In fact, it's just been in the last few months that I really started to have a closer walk with the Lord. I started praying—certain things—and still am. That's when everything began to happen."

The spark of interest generated by Andy's last statement flamed into rapt attention, as his listeners leaned forward expectantly. "One morning this past July I asked God to forgive me for not being a better witness. I confessed that I'd been a Christian for years and hadn't won many souls to the Lord."

His eyes met Tom's. "I'd heard about God's promise in Joel to restore the years that the locusts had eaten and I asked the Lord to let the locusts eat up all my barren years. It was about a week after that—that Evie—was taken." Tears glistened in his eyes and one ran down his cheek.

The stunned group waited as the minutes seemed to stretch into hours before Andy spoke again. "I've also begun to pray that God would give me a tremendous hunger and thirst for the Word of God, as well as a desire to be obedient to the Lord and live close to Him. And He has. The Lord has been working in my life and I *know* that some of my desires and goals have changed. My main goal today is that I do *exactly* what He wants me to do. It's not so important what *I* want to do, but it's important that I do what *He* wants. It's important that I accomplish *His* purpose in my life."

"Amen. I want that to always be my goal, too," agreed Tom. "There's nothing more important than following the Lord and obeying His commands."

Prayer followed, and with it, a time of renewed commitment to doing the Lord's work in the Lord's way.

Ruth's mind whirled with the fears and doubts that Andy's testimony had touched off. Sudden silence brought her to the realization that it was her turn to pray. As if at some distance she heard herself begin, "Our heavenly Father, we thank you for our Lord Jesus Christ—"

89

THURSDAY

OCTOBER 9, 1980

Chapter Ten

Thursday—October 9, 1980

A yellow rosebud curled into delicate peaks under Ruth's skillful hands. Set in a bed of soft pink and white petals and garnished with swirling green leaves, the floral artistry concealed luscious layers of chocolate cake underneath.

As Ruth placed her handiwork on a shelf, she wondered whether another Thursday would ever pass without her remembering her last conversation with Evie. Would she ever forget her last words: "I'm going now." Once more she could see Evie as she walked out of the kitchen that last Thursday on her way to an appointment with—with what?

Ruth found herself still standing with her hands touching the sides of the pan she had just set on the shelf. How long had she been daydreaming about the past? "This will never do. I must concentrate on what I'm doing *now*— here at the bakeshop," she reminded herself.

It wasn't long until "Happy Birthday" was penned with sugary ink across another freshly baked dessert. Ruth gave it an approving glance. She found that using her creative talents helped to overcome the feelings of despair which accompanied her every waking moment.

Visits like that with the Taylors last night helped, too. Through them, memories of the past were at least partially replaced with the reality of the present. And the present, no matter how empty, was all she had.

She was so absorbed in her work that she didn't notice Andy quietly walk into the shop. Turning to get another tube of icing, she was startled to see him standing almost at her elbow. One look at his face told her. There was news in the search for Evie.

She squeezed the tube convulsively. The green leaf on the cake became a shapeless lump of colored sugar. Trying to control her shaking hand she scraped away the leafy failure and replaced it with an impatient flourish.

"Here, hon, I'll put the cake away while you clean the table. Junior's out in the car waiting for us," Andy said.

Ruth had never seen Andy's face so drawn, so tense. The fear that engulfed her had its roots deep within her. Her body trembled like ripples on a stream. They had found Evie. And she wasn't alive. The tiny flame of hope was about to be snuffed out.

Mechanically she followed Andy out to the parking lot. As he opened the car door, she noticed Junior's unusually serious countenance. He permitted only a suggestion of a smile as he turned to greet her with a quiet, "Hi, Mom." Andy joined her in the back seat and Ruth waited for the inevitable. Time hung suspended.

The car inched toward the street, but Ruth didn't notice. She was only aware of Andy's words—unwanted words that pounded into her mind and reverberated in her heart.

"They've found Evie. She was in the mountains about four miles from our home. She wasn't in the landfill after all."

"Not in the landfill—not in the landfill!" The relief she ached to feel was cruelly squelched as other words echoed in her mind: "in the mountains." She was in the mountains! Every breath stamped the harsh reality on her senses— Evie was dead!

Overwhelming pain and hopelessness flowed through her like waves crashing relentlessly, pounding their way into her heart. The ride from the shop to their home wasn't long enough to shed all the tears.

Stumbling out of the car, Ruth sobbed, "Why, God? Why? You were able to part the waters of the Red Sea and save the children of Israel! Where were you when Evie needed you? Why didn't you help *her*?"

At the sight of Davy clutching his stuffed roadrunner, she stifled her outburst and scooped him into her arms. Pressing him tightly against her body she was aware of his warmth. She felt his every movement and listened to his innocent chatter—wonderful signs of life that she had not appreciated before.

She had no idea how long she stood holding her little son. Time was of no concern to her now. It was meaning-less. There would be no day or hour when she would ever see Evie's bright smile or hear her carefree laughter again. She did not move until she saw Kathy running toward her with outstretched arms, tears streaming down her face.

Later, she watched her daughter set the table. "How will Evie's death affect her? And Terry. He's at work and still doesn't know."

Suddenly the weight of her responsibilities as a mother pressed open a door that allowed new determination to creep into her and plant its seed in her mind. She must try to be strong for the sake of her family.

Feeling Andy's hand on her shoulder, she turned and threw her arms around him. Looking into his eyes she murmured, "At least it's over!" She could feel herself gaining a measure of courage as she yielded to his sympathetic hug. There was a calmness about Andy that she couldn't explain. He seemed to be reaching into some inner resource and gathering a harvest of strength.

Clearing the table not long afterwards, she wasn't surprised that the food was almost untouched. She was wiping the table when Andy's brother and his wife walked into the kitchen. For a moment no one spoke. Andy's brother, Ike, twisted his cap in his hand while Amanda kissed Ruth lightly on the cheek.

Andy broke the silence by motioning to the table. "Have a seat. I want to share something with you that I haven't even told Ruth yet."

The scraping sound of chairs on the linoleum was the only audible response to his suggestion. They waited for him to begin.

"Today," Andy slowly revealed, "God answered prayer in a marvelous way. I've never made it a practice to take a break during my working hours. But this morning I did. Alone with my Bible I read, 'Establish my footsteps in Thy Word, and do not let any iniquity have dominion over me."[1] Then I turned to Hebrews 4:16: 'Let us therefore draw near with confidence to the throne of grace, that we may receive mercy and find grace to help in time of need.'[2]

"I claimed that promise, then I read the account of the demons that Jesus had cast out of a maniac. These devils, as they were called, begged Him not to cast them into the lake, but into a nearby herd of swine. And He did."[3]

Andy looked at each of his listeners, making sure he had their full attention. "Well, I reasoned that if the Lord answered the request of demons, surely He would answer my prayer. I reminded Him that I was one of His children. I admitted that I was not always what I should be, but I *was* one of His! I shared with Him that I felt a critical time had come. The searchers were discouraged, and the number of volunteers at the landfill had dwindled since we had refused the help of psychics. Something had to be done!"

Ruth reached for Andy's hand, silently urging him to continue. After they exchanged glances, he went on. "I made a specific request. I prayed, 'If Evie is in the landfill don't let the searchers give up and leave. But if she is not in there, let today be the last day they search there. Let her be found' "

The tension around the table could be felt as Andy pointed to the clock and said, "My prayer was sometime between the hours of 10:00 and 11:00 this morning. Early this afternoon I was informed that Evie had been found."

Ruth could hear the excitement in Ike's voice as he exclaimed, "Praise the Lord! The mountain area had already been searched many times. God must have given direct guidance!"

Nodding in agreement, Andy explained that Rod

97

Hartman had been scouring the mountains again around noon when he found himself on a fire trail that he hadn't expected to use.

"Something seemed to tell him to continue on the trail," Andy said. "But it wasn't long until he felt compelled to leave it and walk through underbrush so thick that he had to mark it in order to find his way back."

Andy stared into space and bit his lip. "At one point, as he pushed the thick growth aside, he found—he found a skel—" His voice broke. Tears rolled down his cheeks as he visibly tried to compose himself, "—a skeleton. It was Evie—with her hands still tied behind her back."

Now the sobs of the others mingled with his.

Swallowing hard and clenching his fists, he painfully shared what he couldn't keep to himself. "There's still a black outline on the ground where she was lying."

Ruth wasn't sure what that meant. Right now it was almost too much to comprehend that her daughter was dead. In her mind, she saw her Evie being bound, perhaps raped, and murdered. She screamed in anguish.

FRIDAY
OCTOBER 10, 1980

Chapter Eleven
Friday—October 10, 1980

Ruth threw back the covers. Finally, the long sleepless hours of this night had been banished by the first rays of the sun. But as she dressed and made breakfast, she soon discovered that the nightmare of the day before was still with her. Although she outwardly responded to words of sympathy, she was aware of the inner ache that wouldn't be comforted.

Somehow the day passed and soon it was evening again. She glanced at the clock. The undertaker should be here at any moment. The police had said they needed Evie's remains for "an undisclosed amount of time" in order to examine them for evidence. Because of that, there was no way of knowing when the funeral would be. Even so, arrangements had to be made.

Seeing Mr. Furman, a Leola funeral director, and his

wife enter the kitchen, Ruth lost the apprehension she had felt. Their kind manner and concerned attitude dispelled her misgivings about this meeting.

Andy still appeared uneasy, however, and Ruth thought she knew why. The police had chosen someone to remove Evie's remains from the mountain, but Ruth and Andy did not know who it was. Andy had prayed for wisdom in the selection of an undertaker, and in making the funeral arrangements. They wanted their daughter to be handled gently and with respect, and would have preferred to choose an understanding Christian for the task.

Thus, it was two astonished and thankful parents who heard this quiet, unassuming man say that it was *he* who had gone up the mountain to pick up Evie's remains.

Overwhelmed at the guidance God had given, Andy exclaimed, "Praise the Lord!" as he shook the man's hand. "I want to thank you in Jesus' name for what you have done."

They were unprepared for his quiet reply. "It was in Jesus' name that I picked up your precious daughter."

No more words were needed. And for a few minutes none were spoken.

*   *   *

It was midnight. The necessary funeral arrangements had been made.

"You know, Ruth, I've hardly slept since Evie's remains were found and yet I'm not that tired. I feel as if I don't need sleep!" Pausing a moment, Andy reflected, "Maybe I've kept going in the strength of the Lord."

When Ruth didn't answer, he half chuckled, "I don't even have to yawn!"

Wearily, Ruth lay down and turned to face her husband.

A feeling of security enveloped her as he held her in his arms. Quietly, Andy spoke aloud, " 'Do not fret because of evildoers, be not envious toward wrongdoers.' "[1]

As his voice faded away, an indescribable peace began to flood the room and fill their hearts. Ruth could hear the awe in Andy's voice as he whispered, "Isn't this marvelous? It seems as if God is right here with us. I can actually sense His presence!"

Now it was Ruth who was in awe. After all her doubts, she, Ruth Fisher, could also sense the very presence of God!

They were both quiet for a long time. Finally, Andy confided, "I wish we could lay here until morning, just enjoying Him!" In the end, however, they succumbed to human frailty and sleep overtook them.

Even so, weeks later, Ruth nodded in agreement as Andy recalled, "The most peaceful night I ever spent in my life."

MONDAY

OCTOBER 13, 1980

Chapter Twelve

Monday—October 13, 1980

"Davy! Look out! There goes your milk! Why can't you be more careful?"

Seeing the puzzled look in her little son's eyes, Ruth became aware of the irritability in her voice. As she wiped the floor she realized it wasn't the spilled milk that had caused her short-tempered reaction. It was the decision she had made when she awoke that morning. Four days had passed since Evie's body had been found and she had decided to face the unpleasant job of sorting through Evie's belongings. A few to keep. Most to give away. She dreaded the emotional ordeal it involved.

Reaching for Davy as he finished his cereal, Ruth gave him a repentant hug. In return, he threw his arms around her neck and planted a wet kiss on her cheek.

"Davy, Davy!" she murmured. "Whatever would I do

without you?"

As he ran to play with his cars and trucks, Ruth climbed the stairs to the girls' room. She'd begin with Evie's clothes, she decided. Her hand was on the closet door when she spied a partly opened bureau drawer. A brightly colored book caught her eye. Ruth gasped as she recognized an almost forgotten treasure—Evie's *Triumphant Teen Devotional Book.*

Memories flooded her mind as she clasped the precious diary in her hands. For an instant she was back in the Life Action services in their church, remembering the commitments that had been made to the Lord and the wrongs that had been righted. During those four weeks at Twin Valley Bible Chapel, the Holy Spirit had worked mightily in many hearts and had changed lives. Evie had been in those services two years ago. The notations she had made in this daily account stemmed from that time.

Reflectively, Ruth turned the pages to the first entry. Excitement seized her as she realized that she was about to glimpse what had been in her daughter's teenage heart and mind in the months just preceding her departure. She could almost hear Evie's voice as she read the familiar handwriting: "I should let God have His way with me. God will be my helper. God is in control. Jesus loves His sheep."

" 'Jesus loves His sheep.' Then, *why*, Lord? Why did you allow this to happen?"

Unbidden sobs convulsed Ruth. For how many minutes she yielded to their control, she didn't know. But somewhere in the back of her mind she began to hear Andy's words: "What? *What* are you trying to show us? What purpose does all this have?" Slowly her sobs subsided.

Gradually, she discovered the inner strength to continue her pursuit.

Paging through several other entries she found that Evie had determined to live "by letting God have me, letting God lead me." She had reminded herself: "When I know what God wants me to do, do it." Her desire had been to "help me live His Word, not just read it. Help me witness to people; help me to be kind and loving to everybody."

The next petition caused Ruth to stop and stare in disbelief: "Protect me from Satan."

Evie—innocent, naive Evie! Wanting to help others—unsuspecting. Indeed, where *was* her protection? Ruth stopped. She must not entertain bitter thoughts against God!

It was with a rush of relief that her eyes fastened on a scrawled entry: "I praise Him that I am saved." She caught her breath. Evie had spoken of being saved when she was a pre-schooler, but the details were hazy in Ruth's mind. Now, here it was—*written down*!

Bowing her head, she thanked the Lord for this tangible evidence. Evie had felt that all was well with her soul! Gratitude overwhelmed her and tears rolled down her cheeks. She, Ruth, might still have personal doubts, but Evie *knew*. And Evie had needed to know.

Carefully placing a marker at that page she turned to another entry she would share later with Andy: "I'm thankful for good Christian parents who told me about God." There had been times Andy and she had questioned their actions and reactions with their children. Were they really "bringing them up in the nurture and admonition of the Lord"?[1] Here was the reassurance they needed.

Continuing to read, she found that Evie had been

109

thankful "for God's love to me, and that He is able to do all things." She had been especially thankful that "He kept me safe." What was Evie referring to?

A trace of a smile crossed Ruth's face. Maybe it was from a dog! Except for their own animals, Dixie and Sparkie, Evie had been afraid of dogs. Not without cause. When she was about two years old, they had "dog-sat" their pastor's German shepherd for several days. He loved to chase the older children, and Evie had wanted him to chase her, too. Finally, one day her wish was granted. She laughed and screamed as she enjoyed the merry chase. But upon catching up with her, the dog's greeting was more forceful than she had expected. Jumping on her with all four feet, he had knocked her down and tried to lick her. Petrified, poor Evie had passed out! From then on, except for the family's dogs, she had stayed a respectful distance away from members of the canine family.

" 'He kept me safe,' " Ruth repeated. Evie had been afraid, too, of riding her bicycle alone. A grocery store was only a few blocks from their house, yet she had ridden there only two or three times. Of what—or whom—was Evie afraid?

Still preoccupied with Evie's fears, Ruth idly flipped the pages one more time. It was a relief to see Evie's humor in evidence throughout the book with drawings of birds, hearts, and flowers. There was even a comical sketch of a fish wearing a hat! More serious was the heart with an arrow piercing it, linking a certain boy at her school with her own name!

Near the end, a page contained her signature written several different ways. "Evelyn. . .Evie. . .Evie Fisher. . .Evie Marie Fisher."

"That was my girl," Ruth muttered as she carefully placed the book back into the drawer. Then with sudden insight, she added, "No, that *is* my girl!"

Walking into the kitchen, she knew, "Whichever way it's written, her name is in the Lamb's Book of Life."

WEDNESDAY
OCTOBER 15, 1980

Chapter Thirteen

Wednesday—October 15, 1980

A branch narrowly missed scraping Ruth's face before she pushed it aside and reached for another protruding twig. Each step was marked by the crunch of dried leaves. The only other sound was an occasional bird calling its messages to whatever creatures were listening.

No one spoke. Ruth turned and glanced at Alma who was picking her way through the thick underbrush. Behind her, Hiram was holding a scarlet-leafed limb aside for his wife, Fay. At another time, and another place, she and Andy would have enjoyed hiking through the autumn woods with their friends. Hilarity and laughter would have followed them along the almost hidden trail. Instead, there was grim-faced silence.

Ruth didn't notice that Andy had stopped until her foot caught on a hidden root and she staggered against him.

Her eyes followed his to the grayish outline of Evie's body on the fallen leaves. Now all footsteps were silent and, kneeling with an almost reverential awe, the quiet group stared at the repulsive pattern before them. No one mentioned the musty odor that permeated the air. The sound of tears communicated their emotions.

Overhead, the trees formed a golden canopy lit by the dancing rays of the late afternoon sun. On the ground, tears dampened the dusky leaves where Evie's body had lain.

Ruth felt resentment and anger take control. Her muscles tightened in response to their onslaught. Then Andy spoke. Astonished, Ruth heard him say, "I want all of you to give up your bitterness and resentment against the person that did this. This is important for what I have to share later."

Ruth's heart protested. Why *shouldn't* she feel resentment toward the person who had done this to her daughter? Yet, she sensed the urgency in his voice. So much had already happened. Could Andy know events that none of the rest of them had yet been told? Fear gripped her anew. Somehow she managed to push it out of her mind as Andy began to pray.

Prayers of confession and petition emanated from the hearts of her four companions. And, as the autumn foliage reached up to touch the clear blue sky, their prayers reached even higher to touch the throne of God Himself. Ruth's heart softened and she gave over to the Lord all the resentment she felt for the one she suspected of harming her daughter.

After the last "Amen" had been uttered, Andy struggled to verbalize what Ruth had been afraid to ask since Evie's remains had been discovered. "We've all been—hoping—that she died quickly—of a sudden blow."

Horrible as that image was to her mother's heart, Ruth kept her eyes focused steadily on Andy as he slowly and painfully continued.

"But information has been received that she *did* suffer first—that she was beaten while she was tied."

A scream resounded in the autumn woods. Then hysterical sobs. Then silence. And in those moments of silence, other screams penetrated Ruth's mind: Evie's first cries at birth; her call for help as a dog jumped on her; her shriek of alarm as she was pulled from the path of a truck; her squeals of delight as Davy was placed in her arms for the first time. And she could imagine Evie's screams of pain and terror when she was beaten.

THURSDAY
OCTOBER 16, 1980

Chapter Fourteen

Thursday—October 16, 1980

It was Thursday again, one week since Evie had been found. Ruth had returned home from the bakeshop, made lunch for the family, and folded the clothes that Kathy had washed and dried. Davy had fallen asleep on her lap and she took advantage of the opportunity to stay seated for awhile.

Trying not to disturb him, she removed a pink notebook from her apron pocket. The cover pictured a girl and her cat, along with the words, "You're Nice 2 Be With." It was the notebook in which Evie had written chapel notes while attending Leola Christian School.

With the ordeal of the day before still oppressing her, Ruth sought what comfort she could find from Evie's written words. Opening the notebook expectantly she found the notation: "We are on the winning side.

There is honor and glory coming to the people who live for God." This was followed by the caution: "The Christian life is not all fun. There is a lot of suffering."

Eagerly Ruth reached for her Bible to read the references which followed Evie's comments. "Now I want you to know, brethren, that my circumstances have turned out for the greater progress of the gospel."[1] Why—this was Andy's desire, too, that souls would be saved because they heard the gospel through Evie's death!

Noting that Evie also referred to another verse, Ruth read: "For to you it has been granted for Christ's sake, not only to believe in Him, but also to suffer for His sake."[2] Slowly she repeated, "not only to believe. . .but also to suffer. . . ."

"Evie!" she exclaimed aloud. "Could I claim this verse for you? You believed on the Lord Jesus Christ. You suffered the hurt, the humiliation, the horror of being attacked and beaten to death."

Through misty eyes Ruth read the ending again, "for His sake." For His sake. *Suffering. . .for His sake.* She had always associated suffering with being a martyr, maybe a missionary, who dies for the cause of Christ. Was it possible it could relate to Evie, too?

Ruth agonized in her thoughts, "Oh Evie, I often think of the times when I had doubts and tried to persuade you not to go clean for Gary, but you wanted to earn the money and assured me that I had nothing to fear. He had somehow convinced you that he was a Christian and wouldn't harm you! I guess he had convinced me, too. He even went to church with us once. You and I were both blind.

"Yet, you should have listened to my request that you

122

not go. In fact, Daddy and I should have forbidden you to go over there."

Even though Ruth had been sincere in giving up her resentment as they had prayed at the mountain site the day before, she suddenly felt a new surge of hostility. "But you went, Evie. And you learned in a moment of time that the world is filled with hatred, lust and selfish desires that will seek to take by force, if necessary, that which it covets." Suddenly aware of her clenched fists, Ruth opened her hands, smoothed Davy's hair and straightened his rumpled shirt.

Still talking to Evie in her thoughts, Ruth went on, "But when you discovered his intent, I know you struggled against the lustful, ungodly acts which he had planned. But the strength and skill which you had admired overcame you, and soon you were bound and beaten, wrapped in a blanket, heading for you knew not where."

Ruth closed her eyes, as if to blot out the mental picture she had painted. But it only appeared more clearly because recent information supplied by the police was still burning in her mind. "Somehow you managed to struggle upright in the back of your abductor's car and scream for help. You probably had hope that you could still reason with the man you thought he was! You begged him to let you out! But you felt his response with his fists rather than heard his voice. His deceptively convincing manner was abandoned now. Brute force took over."

Ruth stood up to lay Davy in his crib before her agitated movements could awaken him. She stroked his hands and cheeks absentmindedly as she finally permitted questions which tortured her to formulate in her mind: "Did he wait to stuff your sock down your throat until he reached the mountain trail? Were you conscious as he cut off your clothes? Were you still alive when he left you?"

Tears flowed down Ruth's cheeks as she stumbled back to the security of her chair. Aloud, she determined, "Yes, Evie, your suffering *was* for His sake."

Picking up her still open Bible, she began to read again and was comforted.

SATURDAY

OCTOBER 18, 1980

Chapter Fifteen

Saturday—October 18, 1980

The day had finally arrived. Ruth pushed a strand of hair back from her face. This was Evie's day. Her dark eyes grew moist as the dream of her daughter walking down the church aisle as a bride faded into the reality of a casket being carried down the aisle instead.

Somehow, maybe out of respect for her daughter, she felt compelled to look her best. Peering into a mirror, Ruth carefully inspected her appearance. Seeing that the new black dress with its floral print was hanging in neat folds, and brushing her hair one more time, she picked up her purse and hurried into the kitchen.

Andy was getting Davy his last drink of water before leaving for the funeral. As Ruth passed the hutch, she noticed the enlarged photo of Evie which had been placed on Evie's closed coffin the night before for the "viewing."

At the funeral home Ruth had met some of the searchers for the first time. Entire units from fire companies had filed past in uniform, paying their respects. What an encouragement it had been to see those who cared and had freely given of their time to help someone in need.

Feeling a tug at her dress, Ruth looked down into Davy's inquiring eyes. Quickly she took his hand and hurried to the waiting car.

*   *   *

The sight of the petite casket in the spacious foyer of the familiar red brick church pierced Ruth's heart. The outside of the coffin was white for purity and innocence. Inside was a skeleton covered with last year's frilly Easter dress and Sunday shoes. "Think about her dress and shoes when you look at the casket," the undertaker had said.

Andy's words reverberated in her ears also. "Think about Evie not being there! She's somewhere else!"

Ruth was barely aware of the scurrying to and fro of ushers and personnel from the local Christian radio station. She felt detached from the hushed voices of sympathizing friends and relatives. As Andy's strong hand guided her down the aisle to the front pew, she felt that time was standing still.

She had been seated but a moment when she became conscious of an inner change that seemed ready to burst forth, grow, and mature. It was a moment of new insight and strengthened purpose in her life, a time from which all future moments would emanate.

Like ointment poured on a wound, organ music filled the church with its soothing notes of hope and peace. Unexpectedly, anticipation gripped her. She, Ruth, was in need of receiving a message from the Lord. And she was ready to receive it. In her mind she could still see Andy giving Davy a drink of water to satisfy his thirst before they left home. Now she felt—no, she *knew*—that her heavenly Father was about to satisfy the spiritual thirst that had been tormenting her since Evie's disappearance.

Tears fell unbidden as the first strains of "Safe in the Arms of Jesus" echoed throughout the sanctuary. That's where her Evie was today—safe with the Lord. The notes continued to permeate the auditorium.

Safe—in Jesus—safe—in JESUS! Ruth's heart wanted to burst with joy! *She* was safe in Jesus, too! She was apart from Him; Evie was at home with Him. Still He loved and cared for them both.

As the majestic notes of "Great Is Thy Faithfulness" filled the air, Ruth prayed, "Thank you, Lord. You've been giving me the strength to face this ordeal. I've been doubting, but all the while you've been with me, showing yourself faithful to me—and loving me!"

Her shoulders shook. She attempted to hold back her sobs as the organist's next song caused her to mentally verbalize the message: "I must tell Jesus. I cannot bear my burdens alone. I must tell Jesus. Jesus can help me. Jesus alone."

Raising her head, a determined smile tasted the salty tears coursing down her face. Hope filled her with joy from above. She knew. Her heart sang: "When the roll is called up yonder I'll be there. . .when time shall be no more and the morning breaks eternal, bright and fair."

She wanted to shout her praise: "I am 'redeemed by the blood of the Lamb. His child and forever I am! Redeemed—and so happy in Jesus!' "

The peace that flooded Ruth's soul was not dependent upon earth's joys or sorrows. Rather, it produced a tranquility that helped her soar above the worst that this earth could do to her.

She whispered with the next hymn, "My Jesus, I love Thee. I *know* Thou art mine."

Soon the service opened with Pastor Dick's prayer. "Our precious Father, we thank you for the opportunity that you give to us moment by moment to enter into the very throne room of God. We thank you for the way that has been provided through Thy Son, Jesus Christ. And we ask, our Father, now as we gather at this funeral service in memory of Evelyn Fisher, that you minister to our hearts. . . ."

"Thank you, Father, for already ministering to my heart," Ruth breathed. "Thank you."

After their pastor's prayer, Ruth fervently sang with the congregation, "Amazing grace, how sweet the sound. . .I once was blind, but now I see—"

This new peace comforted her sorrowing spirit as the pastor reminded those present that, "We're gathered together in memory of a loved one, Evelyn M. Fisher, who was born on September 8, 1965, and entered into her eternal rest on July 31, 1980 at the age of 14 years, 10 months, and 23 days."

He was speaking of the death of her daughter, her own flesh and blood. Ruth had to accept the fact that Evie was gone. Mentally and emotionally she had to give her up. She could no longer cling to a false hope.

Slowly she became aware that her eyes were fastened on the cross which dominated the baptistry and towered above the pulpit. She began to comprehend the suffering—

and love—involved in another death over nineteen hundred years before. The death of God's Son, Jesus Christ. God the Father had willingly given Him up. He had given His Son to die for Ruth Fisher—and for Evie!

An imperceptible nod of agreement answered the pastor's question, "Was Evie ready to go?" A smile tugged at the corners of her mouth as he reminded the mourners that Evie had received Christ as her personal Saviour and, because of that decision, she was with the Lord today.

Andy's words rang in Ruth's ears once more—words she had heard him repeat over and over during the search, words which, until today, had brought frustration rather than comfort to her heart: "If she's not here on earth, we know where she is. She's in Heaven with the Lord Jesus."

Looking again at the casket, Ruth knew that she'd see Evie again. Evie was in Heaven. And she, Ruth, was going there, too. She was sure of it now!

Even as she rejoiced in her newfound assurance, she heard Pastor Dick continue, "Evelyn has gone on to be with the Lord. But what about us? Where are we going? Where will our eternal destiny be?"

Since that question was now settled in Ruth's heart and mind, she found herself thinking about friends and relatives who were sitting in the pews behind her, some of them unsaved.

"Oh, Lord," she silently prayed, "speak to their hearts. May someone come to know you as Saviour during this service. In Jesus' name I pray, Amen."

The message continued. "There are two types of people here today—those who are saved and those who are lost. In the third chapter of the Gospel of John we read that 'He

131

that believeth on the Son hath everlasting life; and he that believeth not the Son shall not see life; but the wrath of God abideth on him."[1]

"It doesn't say anywhere in the Word of God that membership in a church, baptism, or sincerity will get us into Heaven.

"In Romans 3, we are reminded that 'All have sinned and come short of the glory of God.' In chapter six we read that 'the wages of sin is death, but the gift of God is eternal life."[2]

"In Ephesians, chapter two, we are told that 'by grace are ye saved through faith; and that not of yourselves: it is the gift of God: Not of works, lest any man should boast."[3]

"My friends, today on behalf of Andy and Ruth, I extend to you the offer of receiving Christ as Saviour. It is their desire that you might come to know the Lord in a very personal way. Jesus said, 'I am the way, the truth, and the life: no man cometh unto the Father, but by me.'"[4]

Thankfulness welled up in Ruth's heart as she thought again of all the Lord Jesus had done for her. He loved *her* so much that He took her punishment and died on the cross for *her* sins. Because of this, He was able to offer her the free gift of salvation—if she would receive Him as her own personal Saviour. And she had! She was certain now. She had acknowledged that she was a sinner, and had responded in faith to Him years ago. But doubts had robbed her of peace and joy many times. Now she accepted what she had known long ago: "It is enough that Jesus died—and that He died for *me!*" The words of this forgotten song came from deep in Ruth's memory and stamped an *amen* on her reaffirmed faith.

During the pastor's invitation, her own heart overflowed

with a prayer of gratitude. "Oh, Lord Jesus, thank you—thank you for saving me! Thank you for giving me the assurance today that I'll see Evie again in Heaven."

Tears of rejoicing filled Ruth's eyes as several hands were raised, indicating their desire to receive Christ as their personal Saviour. She bowed her head as Pastor Dick urged them to pray with him: "Father, forgive me of my sin. I ask you to come into my heart as my Saviour and Lord. Thank you, Lord Jesus, for saving me and giving me eternal life. In Jesus' name I pray, Amen."

And then, the first triumphant strains of "Victory in Jesus" flowed from the piano, organ, and brass instruments. Overwhelmed with the restored joy of her salvation, Ruth gazed at the coffin and whispered from the private recesses of her heart, "Oh, Evie, I know I'll see you again! One day I'll be joining you and we'll spend all eternity together!"

* * *

Dark, ominous clouds overtook the long procession of cars as it approached Lancaster. While they followed the hearse mile after mile, Ruth saw another procession in her mind's eye: that of the sinless Saviour, carrying His cross to Calvary. He had felt the pain of death. He knew the agony of suffering.

Suddenly, one of the heaviest downpours Ruth had ever been in unleashed torrents of water upon them. Almost blinded by the deluge, they carefully made their way through the streets of the city. But by the time the last of the procession had reached the cemetery, the cloudburst had dwindled to a gentle, steady rain.

Umbrellas extended beyond the canopy onto adjoining

133

gravesites as the service began. As they had requested, Pastor Dick read Psalm 34, the Scripture passage Ruth had been reciting when Evie was born into the world. These were the same verses Evie's principal had assigned as memory work at the academy this fall—verses Evie would have memorized had she lived. Today Ruth had experienced verse 4: "I sought the Lord, and He answered me, and delivered me from all my fears."[5] She was no longer afraid of dying. She was saved, and she knew it!

Yet, at the sight of the lonely white coffin perched atop its resting place, feelings of grief and helplessness still engulfed Ruth. Tears rolled down her cheeks. But Jesus shared even this. He had wept at Lazarus' tomb. He, too, had experienced the sorrow of death. She didn't weep alone.

She knew that Jesus had won the victory over this enemy, death. He had arisen from the tomb; and one day Evie would arise in a glorified body, clothed in immortality.

But for now, an empty void was left inside Ruth. No one in all her remaining life on earth would be able to fill that special place in her heart that was Evie's. Gone were the loving touch, the intimate conversation, the fond sharing of memories, and aspirations for the future. None of them existed anymore—not even in the little white coffin.

THURSDAY
NOVEMBER 27, 1980

Chapter Sixteen

Thursday—November 27, 1980

The tantalizing odor rising from the skillet on the stove blended with the taste-tempting aroma escaping from the oven. Ruth smiled with approval at the browning turkey. One more basting should do it. It would be moist and golden by noon.

As she glanced at the clock she heard footsteps behind her. "Be careful, Davy. It's hot!" she cautioned as a tousled head peered hungrily at the turkey.

"Is it time to eat?" Davy's hopeful eyes looked up at his mother.

"No, sleepy head," Ruth laughed, "but it won't be long. I'll pour you a glass of orange juice and some cereal to help you wait!"

Munching his corn flakes, Davy eyed his mother's every move as she tossed a mountain of bread cubes with other ingredients.

"It's Thanksgiving, Davy, and we're going to have a luscious meal!" Ruth's voice caught as she glanced at her youngest child. Momentarily her vision blurred. For an instant she saw the dark luminous eyes, the ready smile, and the shining black hair of another pre-schooler who had always been near when mother was in the kitchen—a daughter who was absent today. The rush of memories threatened to overwhelm Ruth as she placed the savory stuffing in the baking dish. But, at the sound of Davy's spoon scraping his empty bowl, she turned and saw today's child—living, demanding, in need of his mother's love and concern. Ruth dropped her spoon and held him close.

*   *   *

There! The last piece of pumpkin pie was sliced and ready to serve. Ruth took a deep breath. This would be the time to suggest her idea. She had everyone's attention. Trying to sound as positive as she could, she began, "After the dishes are cleared away, let's all go into the living room—"

Junior interrupted with a groan, "Aw, Mom, I was going to ride my motorcycle this afternoon."

"I was going to see if Nancy and Kathy Overly are home—after the dishes are done, of course." Kathy dropped her eyes to avoid Ruth's.

"I thought I'd—" Terry stopped when he saw the imploring look his mother directed at Andy who, in turn, held up his hand for silence.

"I don't see any reason why we can't all spend some time together as a family today," Andy remonstrated.

"You can visit your friends later if you want."

Ruth detected their dissatisfaction, but, as the pieces of pie were passed around, no one offered another excuse.

Anxious to start, Ruth began to clear the table as soon as the plates were empty. She said, in what she hoped was a convincing tone, "Let's go to the family room. We'll do the dishes later. Watch where you walk. Davy built a highway of cars and trucks around the coffee table before dinner!"

Soon they were enjoying each other's company, laughing and joking about how much they had just eaten. She was untying her apron as she sat down next to Andy. He reached for her hand and gave it a knowing pat before whispering in her ear, "Everything's going to be all right, hon."

The room became silent. There was a sense of expectancy. The reason for this family time, though unspoken, was obvious: Evie must be included today—even in her absence. Finally, the inevitable question was asked: "Do you remember when. . ." and memories began to perfume the air.

"Remember that tiny dog, Tippy?" Terry laughed. "I think it was a beagle and daschund mixed. Evie used to dress it up and put it in her doll coach. Then she'd push it around as if she had a regular doll instead of a dog!"

Andy chuckled, "It really was your dog, Terry. Sometimes he'd run after you, yelping just like he was chasing a rabbit. Evie would laugh and call out her encouragement—sometimes to you and sometimes to Tippy!

"I remember one afternoon after Tippy died. I was resting because of my early hours at the bakeshop." Andy's eyes gleamed as he leaned forward and continued,

"Evie ran into the bedroom, bubbling with excitement about a little puppy she had seen at Katie's.

" 'You should see that puppy! It's only this long!' she had said, measuring it for me with her hands.

" 'Can we get it? It's *so* cute!' she had pleaded.

"I answered, 'Oh, I don't know.'

" '*Can* we get it?' she had asked again.

" 'Well, *maybe*,' I remember answering.

"That was the wrong thing to say. To Evie it meant yes. And that same week we went to get it.

"I expected to see a cute Doberman puppy, but instead I saw a shabby little mutt with a skin infection and a broken hip! It was *ugly* looking!"

Shaking his head, he recalled, "I spent about sixty dollars at the vet's and Evie gave it all kinds of pills and baths until it began to look like a dog should."

Ruth heard herself add in a tight voice, "Evie couldn't wait for Dixie to grow up and protect her!"

Junior gave his mother a quick glance. His lighthearted response seemed deliberate. "Evie liked to have fun! She'd have merry chases with Terry, Kathy and me— sometimes in dark rooms! We'd bump into furniture and collide with each other until we didn't know where we were."

"Like the time she ended up with a broken collarbone. . . *fun!*" Ruth added drily.

Junior smiled slightly before going on. "The ping pong championship she won at school a couple of years ago was less dangerous. She even beat the boys' champ!" He held his head as if he still couldn't believe the results of that match.

Kathy stopped munching her after-dinner mint and

cleared her throat in a mock threat. But before she could intervene in her sister's defense, Terry recollected, "Evie enjoyed giving you a hard time about eating ice cream, Dad. She'd tease you, even though she liked it, too; almost as much as her favorite food—the bars of chocolate you two shared." He hesitated. "Part of one bar was still in the refrigerator the day she was first missing."

Andy's lips quivered, but he said nothing. Suddenly the atmosphere seemed heavy again.

Only Kathy seemed oblivious to the emotional upheaval. "I can still see her on the Scrambler at the farm show," she shared with a faraway look in her eyes. "It was her favorite ride and she screamed every minute! Then we munched candy apples and ate steak sandwiches.

"One year Evie entered sugar cookies in the local competition and got first prize! I had more experience baking but only got second prize with my red velvet cake."

Sharpness could be detected in Kathy's voice as she continued, "Of course, she had entered in the younger category and I'd competed with older people."

Turning toward her mother, she revealed, "Even though she had used *your* recipe, and was judged differently, she was proud of her first prize. And she let me know it!"

Ruth was unprepared for Kathy's sudden change of attitude. She hadn't realized how Evie's achievement had affected her older daughter.

After sliding to the floor and returning a runaway truck to Davy, Kathy propped against her chair and clasped her hands around her knees as she muttered, "She wasn't always a perfect angel, you know."

Did Ruth imagine the defensive tone in Kathy's voice?

"At school she teased the boy who sat between her and her best friend, Lois. Evie'd take Jim's pencils in retaliation for his tricks on her! And sometimes she and Lois whispered back and forth, trying to annoy him. Then, at Pinchot State Park on the school trip, Lois and she tried to push Jim in the lake, but he pushed Evie in instead!" She grinned at the surprised expressions in the room. "Somehow, she managed to only get one foot wet!"

Grabbing Davy and his ambulance, she held him as she explained, "Evie wasn't mad at Jim, though, because she went to his birthday party just two days before—before—" Her voice trailed off as she rumpled Davy's hair. Amidst his squeals of protest she revealed, "Everyone went out in the woods and told ghost stories. Then the guys ran off with their flashlights and left the girls screaming in the dark."

Pushing a bright yellow truck across the green carpet turf, Kathy mused, "Lois and Evie used to play tennis together." Then, she murmured, "They spent more time sitting under the trees talking than they did playing tennis."

Glancing at her father, Kathy pushed herself back up onto her chair. "Lois said she could always tell Evie her secrets and trust her to keep them to herself. Besides, she said, Evie could always cheer her up." Her voice was barely audible as she noted, "Evie was always laughing."

Seconds passed and no one spoke. Andy provided a welcome relief as his voice cut through the uncomfortable silence. "I've been waiting to share something with all of you. Since Evie's been gone I've picked up her Bible from time to time and read verses that she had underlined—verses like: 'Trust in Him at all times.' "[1] Taking a deep breath, he revealed, "Evie not only underlined those words in Psalm 62, but she wrote 'at all times' again in the margin next to them."

Ruth caught her breath, and the children exchanged quick glances. In response to Andy's request, she handed Evie's Bible to him. He turned to Psalm 56 and half-whispered: " 'When I am afraid, I will put my trust in Thee . . . .In God I have put my trust; I shall not be afraid. What can mere man do to me?' "[2]

Then, turning the pages and passing the Bible to Junior he pointed to Psalm 72:12. His voice was choked as he asked, "Will you read this for me?"

"Sure, Dad. 'For he will deliver the needy when he cries for help, The afflicted also, and him who has no helper.'[3] Did you see the two exclamation marks at the end of that verse?"

"Yes, Evie put them there." Andy's hand trembled as he reached for the precious Bible and gave it to Ruth.

"She was alone that day, and yet not alone." Ruth seemed to be talking to herself. "God was present."

She heard Andy's almost inaudible response. "Praise the Lord. She's not afraid anymore. She's free from all suffering."

Then with unexpected suddenness he jumped up and disappeared into the adjoining room. Seconds later he reappeared with a tape recorder in his hand and a slight smile on his face. Ruth's eyes met Terry's as Andy pushed the button. Could it be—?

The childish voice that rang throughout the room answered her question. "To God be the glory, great things He has done." The song continued with unmistakable clarity and conviction.

Evie's certainty that "Jesus never fails" brought tears to the eyes of those staring transfixed at the little black instrument.

They heard the question, "What can wash away my sin?" They listened to the answer, "Nothing but the blood of Jesus."

Ruth watched the tape winding at its fixed pace. Evie's voice had stopped singing. For a few seconds only the methodical scratching from the tape player could be heard. Then Evie spoke. "And now I'm going to sing, 'O, How I Love Jesus.' And, oh, how I do!"

Muffled sobs accompanied words which had been re-corded almost two years before as they filled the room with sweet assurance.

> *There is a name I love to hear,*
> *I love to sing its worth;*
> *It sounds like music in my ear,*
> *The sweetest name on earth.*
> *Oh, how I love Jesus—*
> *Because He first loved me!*

The familiar song faded away. It had taken on a new meaning. Ruth closed her eyes. She began to sing, "Oh, how I love Jesus." Gradually, other voices joined her.

WEDNESDAY

DECEMBER 17, 1980

Chapter Seventeen
Wednesday—December 17, 1980

Ruth's eyes remained fixed on Gary Newmen. The hearing was over. Spectators were leaving the courtroom, sharing their personal observations with one another in hushed tones. She was aware of Andy's tug on her arm as he stood up. Still she did not move. Gary had left the seat where he had silently watched the proceedings during the two day hearing. It was a stubborn, unrepentant silence, she felt. Now the bitterness that had increased with each testimony reached a crescendo at the sight of the defendant leaving without one word of explanation. Ruth wanted to grab him and shake him until he confessed what he had done. Until he said he was sorry.

And then he turned. For a brief moment his eyes met hers. The sadness and despair that Ruth saw written there melted her resentment and replaced it with unexpected pity.

After directing his gaze at Andy, he was led away. Ruth wanted to call out, "Wait! Can't we talk about it? Just Andy and you and me?" But she had no strength. The violent swing of emotions had left her feeling numb and weak. Her plea remained unspoken.

*   *   *

Neither spoke as they hurried to the car to escape the December chill. Ruth was still shivering as they pulled out of the parking lot adjoining the Lancaster County Courthouse. She was deep in thought as she heard Andy say, "I actually felt sorry for him. That look—I can't describe it!"

Ruth bit her lip and nodded. After a long moment she confided, "I've been feeling bitter again, even justifying my anger, until, until—"

"Until you saw that Newmen is carrying a heavy burden, too. The burden of sin and guilt. Ruth, we musn't stop praying for him. He needs to confess his sin to the Lord and accept Jesus Christ as His Saviour."

Ruth didn't answer. She hadn't been faithful in daily intercession on Gary's behalf.

"It would be to the praise and honor and glory of God if he would be among the redeemed in Heaven. Always remember, Ruth, the blood of Jesus is able to make the vilest sinner clean."

"I'm afraid not everyone understands us, Andy. We—you—talk about God's love and His willingness to save Gary. Yet, at the same time, we want to see justice carried out."

"Ruth, sin shouldn't go unpunished. God doesn't wink

148

at it. In fact, He paid a terrible price because of it." Andy's knuckles turned white as he gripped the steering wheel. "What troubles me is that the law seems to be on the side of the criminal today. I'd like to do all I can to have that changed, even though some tell me to take it easy and not do anything rash!"

"Well, I wouldn't be at all surprised if they hold the trial in another county, probably the western part of the state, to—as they say—'protect the rights of the accused.' But what about the victim's family? Where are our rights? Don't we have any?" Ruth's voice rose in agitation.

"I hope it will be held here in Lancaster County. It will be hard on the little guy if we have to leave him." Lowering his voice, Andy added, "And the older ones are always on my mind, too."

"Sometimes I think they need more supervision than Davy," Ruth sighed. She knew she'd been neglecting Terry, Junior and Kathy lately. Too many days were filled with memories of Evie while she mechanically answered Davy's demands and did routine chores. She loved all of them, but was a personal concern visible? The love in her heart seemed smothered by grief. She was smitten with guilt. She wasn't being fair to her children. They all needed their mother's love. She realized that she must take an interest in the living once again. She must give of herself and become involved in the lives of her remaining family. She must not continue to live in the past.

As the car turned into the driveway, Ruth saw Dixie race across the yard ahead of Terry to greet them. His shiny black head brushed against her as she opened the door. Terry pushed Dixie aside and helped his mother out of the car.

149

"How'd it go today, Mom?" Not waiting for an answer he added, "Wait 'till you see the egg custard I baked while you were gone!"

Ruth squeezed his arm. "Thanks, Terry. Thank you." A warm tear slipped down her cold cheek until her gloved hand wiped it away.

*   *   *

"I'm so glad that Kathy offered to do the dishes tonight. I'm exhausted. I feel emotionally drained."

"Let's go to bed, Ruth." Andy suggested. "We have to get up early tomorrow morning."

"Nooo," Davy interrupted. "Not now," he pleaded.

Andy looked into his little son's imploring eyes and picked him up. "Okay, Davy. We'll sit and talk a little while."

Ruth sighed and put a teakettle of water on the stove. As she pulled mugs from the cupboard and chose tea bags, she listened to the lively chatter between father and son. Davy always had important news to share about the latest episodes with his toys or Dixie.

Sitting with them at the table and sipping the steaming tea, she felt a surge of strength renewing her spirit as well as her body. It wasn't long until Davy squirmed out of his daddy's arms and began to race his cars across the kitchen floor.

"We may as well read some Scripture while we're here, Ruth," Andy suggested as he stirred honey into his tea. "Hand me Evie's Bible, will you?"

At some point in her earthly life Evie had underlined Psalm 40, verses 14 and 17. Andy read it to Ruth. "Let those be ashamed and humiliated together who seek my life to destroy it; Let those be turned back and dishonored who delight in my hurt. . . . Since I am afflicted and needy, Let the Lord be mindful of me, Thou art my help and my deliverer; Do not delay, O my God!"[1]

Ruth pulled the Bible closer and reread the verses while Andy wiped his eyes and blew his nose. Neither spoke.

Taking the Bible from Ruth, Andy's fingers fumbled as he tried to turn to a previously marked page. "I want to show you what she had underlined in Proverbs, Ruth. " '—The wicked will fall by his own wickedness.' "[2]

Ruth nodded her head in agreement. Andy continued, " 'Assuredly, the evil man will not go unpunished, But the descendants of the righteous will be delivered.' "[3]

Ruth remembered their conversation that afternoon concerning justice. "Andy! We don't have to help God!"

"No, Ruth, God will see that judgment is carried out, if not on earth—" He stared at the mug in front of him. His voice sounded abrupt as he suggested, "Let's pray for Newmen's salvation now."

Realizing that the alternative to repentance is eternal death, Ruth prayed as fervently as she could for her daughter's murderer. She wanted to be sincere, but flames of resentment darted in and out of her mind as she petitioned God to convict him of his need of a Saviour. Finally she cried out in desperation, "Oh, God, I'm still harboring feelings of bitterness and hatred within me toward this man. Give me your love and compassion for him! Help me to forgive him."

Sobs shook Ruth's body as Andy held her in his arms. Silently he prayed for his wife.

As her tears subsided, Ruth became aware of a peace that had begun to quiet the turmoil and soothe her frustrations. She managed to smile at Andy and give him a quick hug.

Andy's voice was husky as he told her, "I want to share two more verses with you, hon. They were special to our Evie, and they're going to be cherished by us, too."

Curious, Ruth propped her arms on the table and waited for Andy to find the first reference he had in mind.

" 'Therefore, let those who suffer according to the will of God entrust their souls to a faithful Creator in doing what is right.' "[4]

Radiant hope replaced Ruth's tears of confession from a few minutes earlier. Evie and she had a faithful Creator and Saviour; One to whom they had committed their souls and the One in whose presence Evie was now rejoicing. It was the same One who was giving Ruth a sustaining joy underneath her heartache. A joy that had been absent before the funeral.

As Andy thumbed through the pages, Ruth moved closer to him, eager to see the last verse he had to share. It, too, had been carefully underlined.

"You read it, Ruth," Andy requested.

" 'But let all who take refuge in Thee be glad, Let them ever sing for joy; and mayest Thou shelter them, That those who love Thy name may exult in Thee.' "[5]

"Amen." Andy stood up. "Let's go to bed. God has everything in control."

While Andy helped Davy put his toys away, Ruth read the verse again. As she rinsed the mugs, she repeated aloud: " '—exult in Thee.' "

*   *   *

Andy's regular, even breathing told Ruth that he was asleep. She stretched and savored the wonderful peace that filled her soul. It was the peace of knowing that God understood her fears, and He cared. He knew her frustrations and defeats, yet He loved her. He felt her weakness, and He strengthened her. He had looked upon her darkness and despair, and He had filled her with light and hope.

WEDNESDAY
APRIL 29, 1981

Chapter Eighteen

Wednesday—April 29, 1981

"Okay, hon, I'm ready. Get Davy and let's go!"

Ruth was still in the bedroom when she heard Andy's voice calling from the kitchen. She had made breakfast, washed the dishes, tidied the downstairs, put last minute items in the suitcase for Andy and herself, and made sure that Davy had all the things he needed for the trip. These, of course, included some of his favorite cars and trucks!

Yesterday she had stocked the refrigerator with food for Junior and Kathy who were staying home until they were called to testify. With Terry in the hospital—

Ruth's thoughts were interrupted by a child's voice asking, "Mommy, will Alma let me take these, too?" Davy held an armful of stuffed animals. Ruth laughed at the comical appearance of her little boy clutching toys almost as wide as he was tall!

"Oh, I suppose so! Come along now. You'll have lots of fun with Alma until Mommy and Daddy get back from Easton."

"Why are you going to E—ton?" Davy demanded to know for at least the tenth time.

And, for that many times, Ruth tried to tell him it was because of what had happened to Emmie. She explained that they were going to a trial to talk about Gary Newmen and what he had done to Emmie. Today, as an afterthought, she added, "Now don't you worry about Emmie, Davy. Emmie's in Heaven with the Lord Jesus."

Davy's big brown eyes, which never ceased to melt Ruth's heart, looked up into hers with unquestioning trust as he said, "I know, Mommy. Don't you worry, either."

Soon they greeted Alma, who accepted the appearance of Davy and his toy dogs, bear, lion and roadrunner calmly—even eagerly.

"That's Alma," thought Ruth fondly of her friend. "So kind and patient. I'm thankful that I won't have to worry about Davy while I'm gone. I'll get a little homesick, though." A quick hug and a kiss to Alma, Davy, and the stuffed zoo, and Andy and Ruth were on their way.

* * *

On the highway, Ruth reflected about the needs of her family and committed each of the children to the Lord's care and keeping. She had a God who was able to handle every detail, whether large or small. Now she had to trust Him to do it and not carry her concerns along with her to Easton.

Andy broke the silence. "I was just thinking. I no longer refer to Newmen as Mr. Newmen. I've been searching my heart to see if I'm holding any bitterness toward him. I don't think I am, but neither do I have any respect for someone who sits, refusing to confess or even discuss—what he did to our Evie. With all the evidence that's piled up against him, I couldn't believe it when he entered a 'not guilty' plea in January.

"Besides that, he tried to get some of the most damaging evidence omitted from the trial—the fact that he asked his sister to remove any fingernail clippings from his house and to vacuum his car and wipe it thoroughly."

"Yes," Ruth added, "and he called her from the hospital to ask if she had found any underwear at his place—and whether she had washed all of it!"

Quiet ensued for the next mile as the impact of Newmen's last request hit them with its ugly implication. Finally Andy spoke. *"Now* we know that Newmen told his sister last *September* that he could remember cutting off Evie's shirt—and that she was not at the landfill."

Again, quiet prevailed before Andy commented in a carefully controlled voice, "They've decided to ask for the death penalty."

Ruth's voice rose, "I just pray that justice will be done and that they'll find him guilty of first-degree murder!"

She added in a shaky voice, "I've been praying for Gary's salvation, but I guess I'm not—well, I know I'm not always controlled by the Holy Spirit. Some days I just wish they'd take him out and hang him and get it over with!" There! She'd said it!

Andy measured his response. "I'd say that you really want both things to happen. You'd like to see him accept Jesus Christ as his personal Saviour, and you'd like to see him punished for the crime he committed." Then, in a subdued tone, he agreed, "I think he should get the death penalty, too."

Pulling a New Testament from her purse, Ruth confided, "Andy, I marked two references that Evie had underlined in her Bible. I just remembered them and they're especially appropriate for today. 'Never take your own revenge, beloved, but leave room for the wrath of God, for it is written, Vengeance is Mine; I will repay, says the Lord.' "[1]

Andy nodded, listening intently as Ruth read the second verse. " 'Therefore do not go on passing judgment before the time, but wait until the Lord comes who will both bring to light the things hidden in the darkness and disclose the motives of men's hearts; and then each man's praise will come to him from God.' "[2]

In her mind's eye Ruth saw her daughter's broken body, clothed only with thick underbrush on a deep mountain ridge. She heard the slayer's departing footsteps and the branches rustling as he pushed through the growth to the trail. If he won't tell *now* of his motives and his fatal act, one day it *will* come to light.

The gruesome scene disappeared from before her eyes as Andy commented, "You know that probably no one wants to see justice dealt out in this case more than I do. And as you were reading I realized no matter what the outcome of *this* trial, God the righteous Judge will see that justice *is* meted out—in His time."

Heaving a sigh, he slowly continued, "Ruth, I sense that one thing has been lacking in our conversation—love."

Ruth didn't answer as Andy pulled onto the shoulder and checked the road map. He traced the route with his finger to their northeastern Pennsylvania destination, about sixty-five miles from their home. She felt strangely uneasy as she waited.

Out on the highway once more, Andy mused, "We have to commit this whole trial to the Lord and let Him work out His perfect will. But before we do, we must confess our unloving attitudes toward Newmen and his attorneys, as well as our frustrations toward the judge who moved the trial out of Lancaster County. Only then can we pray that wisdom will be given to the seven men and five women who have been chosen as jurors, to the presiding judge, and to the prosecuting attorneys. Only then can we pray for the strength and courage that each of the witnesses will need."

Somehow, Ruth found herself without words. The magnitude of what they were about to face overwhelmed her. Andy glanced at his frightened wife and reached across the seat to pat her hand. "We also need to pray for ourselves, that the Lord Jesus Christ may be seen in our attitudes and responses. We must be aware of *His* presence with us and experience His sustaining power as we testify and as we witness the proceedings. It's important that we yield to the Holy Spirit's control. If we don't, we will give in to our 'rights,' our tempers, our anger, and our desire for revenge. What we're going to see and hear won't be easy—but He is able to help us even during the hardest moments!"

Still Ruth couldn't speak.

Andy squeezed her hand gently and again tried to comfort her. "Ruth, for some reason God has chosen us to endure this loss and bear this burden. We must remember that. And what we don't understand, we'll try to accept."

She nodded. Tears rolled down her face in a now familiar path.

Reflectively, Andy said, "Ruth, remember the verse that talks about the God of peace perfecting us to do His will, to the glory of Jesus Christ? I think that is one of the things that is happening with us."

Ruth reminded herself more than Andy as she reflected, "God Himself *must* work in us so we're able to do His will. Apart from Him we can't do anything pleasing for Him. Yes, we must pray that we're clean and willing vessels, fit for His use."

Andy nodded in agreement but Ruth didn't notice.

"Why, we can actually look forward to seeing what He is going to do!" she added with a hint of anticipation in her voice.

A slight frown crossed Andy's face. Ruth strained to hear his response. "We must accept whatever He does."

Miles rolled by. Finally, rounding a curve, Ruth spotted the last exit on Route 22 leading to Easton. Looming against the horizon on a distant hillside stood the Northampton County Courthouse.

THURSDAY

APRIL 30, 1981

Chapter Nineteen
Thursday—April 30, 1981

The impressive white columns of the courthouse seemed misplaced in the Pennsylvania surroundings. Yet the hint of southern dignity brightened the appearance of the otherwise busy, pragmatic Yankee town. Even the red sandstone prison which adjoined the courthouse had a quiet, cool air which belied its purpose.

Walking into the courthouse, Ruth attempted to match Andy's careful, deliberate stride. No words were spoken between them, nor did they have to be.

Ruth's heels clicked along the shiny black corridor, silent only when she and Andy rode the elevator the three floors to their destination. As soon as they stepped out of the elevator they were met by such a congenial, elderly gentleman that Ruth's fears diminished. Gratefully, they followed his bright green jacket as he directed them to their seats. Sheaves of papers lay on tables, silent evidence of the preparation which had gone into today's proceedings. All was in readiness.

For an instant she felt as if she were a casual visitor about to observe a drama that was detached from her family or her emotions. The emotional reprieve was short-lived, however. At the sight of the accused ambling to his seat, neatly clad and seemingly at ease, her senses were aroused.

Turning sideways, Ruth saw the jurors begin to enter. She observed them carefully. Through the tears misting her eyes, she silently pleaded with each one. "Oh, please, *please*, listen with sympathy. Please have a tender heart. Please—for Evie—our naive, trusting little Evie."

She watched as they methodically found their assigned seats. The checked jacket, the lavender dress, the blue suit, the flowered skirt; the gray and balding, the blond and brunette. All symbolized the Eventual Decision.

The sound of the gavel brought Ruth to her feet as the judge took his place of authority. She scrutinized this overseer in whose hands so much of the final outcome rested. "Please, Lord, give him wisdom," she whispered.

*   *   *

Today, Andy was the first to testify. Ruth found herself nodding in agreement with his carefully worded responses. Stifling sobs within her, she listened as he recounted their family's activities on that fateful day in July.

His voice broke with emotion as he recalled the pleasant smile that had been characteristic of Evie. His testimony complete, he gazed at the jurors. An inaudible plea seemed to extend from a heartbroken father to the noncommittal eyes of his appraisers.

Weeping, he slowly left the witness stand, seemingly unaware of the quiet sympathy that filled the room. No one moved; no one spoke. He stopped at the water fountain, unable to hide the torment that churned inside and overflowed in agonizing grief. In the silence his anguish intensified, touching even the most callous observers.

Ruth was hardly aware of the next witness. Her thoughts were with Evie, hearing her laughter, seeing her youthful exuberance at the sheer joy of living. Somewhere in the midst of her daydream she heard her name and found herself walking apprehensively toward the witness stand.

As she began to unfold the now familiar story of how she had been shopping with Davy on that unforgettable morning, a middle-aged juror leaned forward, chin in hand. He watched her intently as she told of Evie running out of the house, demanding, "Where were you?"

She managed to tell how Evie and Davy had sat on the kitchen floor and looked at his new socks, admiring the colors. With more difficulty, she recalled how Evie had perched on a stool and eaten lunch with her mother and little brother. Even as she spoke, it seemed ludicrous that such an ordinary event as eating lunch with her daughter would today be of such intense interest to a group of strangers.

Summoning all the courage she could find, Ruth repeated Evie's last words: "I'm going now."

Another juror leaned forward, apparently determined to catch every word, as Ruth added in despair, "And that's the last time I ever saw her."

She sat, biting her lip, fighting to control the hot tears that spilled onto her grief-stricken face. How long did she wait for the next question? It could have been a minute or an hour. Anguish is an inconsiderate time keeper. It stretches seconds of actual pain into hours of reminiscent suffering.

And, *time* was the object of the next question. Yes, she knew when the agonizing drama had begun. It was 12:35 p.m. on July 31st. Her daughter walked out of her life at that moment. That moment was remembered. And so were the hours of fear and worry that had followed for weeks to come.

She told of checking and rechecking Evie's clothing to see what was missing, trying to piece together exactly what she had been wearing when she left. After verifying that Evie didn't take her purse along, she resignedly left the stand, carrying the untouched cup of water which she had taken with her when her name had been called.

Still biting her lip, she managed to retrace her steps below the judge's lofty position, past the defendant who sat stoically between his two counselors.

The touch of Andy's strong hand enfolding hers helped her regain her composure as their daughter, Kathy, made her way to the witness stand.

Casting an apprehensive glance at the jurors, Kathy recounted her activities on that summer afternoon. On arriving home from work, she had decided to go to the neighbor's house where Evie was supposed to be cleaning. Not wanting to scare her sister by walking in unannounced, she had rung the doorbell. Receiving no answer, she had tried the door, only to find it locked. Discovering that the other doors were also locked, she had begun to call Evie's name. Still hearing no answer, she had peered through the closed windows. No one could be seen. While circling the house she'd noticed that the garage door was open and no car was in it.

Ruth shuddered as she visualized Gary's car half-hidden on a mountain trail. She felt Evie's panic as she was yanked out and—. The unbearable picture faded as her daughter stepped down from the witness stand.

Ruth braced herself for the testimony of the next witness. Her dramatic eyewitness account had first been uncovered at the hearing weeks before. Ruth had cringed at the witness' account of the beating Evie had sustained.

Now, once again, the eighty-one year old witness was sworn in. The plainly dressed lady told of sitting in the living room of her home about one-half mile from the Fisher's house on that hot July afternoon. She had been quilting and had all the doors and drapes open. She was quietly concentrating on her sewing, intent on finishing a certain section of her project.

Suddenly she heard a scream, accompanied by loud words she hadn't understood. Thinking perhaps it was children playing at the nearby church nursery school, she walked to the dining room and looked out the window. She could see no teachers or pupils. But what she did see puzzled her. A car was swerving from side to side—and the driver was punching someone on the back seat.

Hurrying outside, she had called, "What's going on out there?" The driver paid no attention. The car stopped on the wrong side of the road next to the widow's mailbox. A girl appeared to lunge over the driver's seat, at which time the man held onto her with one hand and punched her in the face with the other.

Ruth suddenly found it hard to breathe. In her mind, she was back at the preliminary hearing. She saw the aged

169

witness rise from her chair and gesture repeatedly as she described how the driver had used both hands to push someone down behind the back seat. She shuddered at the memory of the witness pointing to Gary Newmen, identifying *him* as the driver of the car.

Returning to the testimony at hand, Ruth heard the woman explain that, in her shock and frustration, she could only think, "Oh, can't I do anything?"

Although visibly moved, the courageous witness painfully continued to share her unnerving experience. The words of the girl haunted her. What had sounded like, "Let me go!" or "Let me out!" caused the elderly lady to hurry from window to window until she saw the car stop again, this time in front of her neighbor's house. In a last attempt to help, she wrote down the license number before the car pulled away and disappeared out of sight. Unfortunately, she mislaid the paper containing the precious information.

Somehow, as she prepared for a trip to the mountains, she was able to dismiss the incident from her mind. It was probably the antics of a drunk couple, she had told herself. But, some time later, rumors of gypsies in the area caused her to remember the strange occurrence in front of her house. Not that the two in the car resembled gypsies, but their actions had been so odd. Should she have reported it to someone? She wondered.

Still indecisive, she found that the memory of that day wouldn't allow her to sleep. At midnight she decided to call her daughter in California and tell her what she had seen. Not long afterward, the police were told the bizarre story.

Tension filled the courtroom as the defense attorney craftily tried to discredit her testimony. More than hints of derision colored his voice as he questioned her memory, her hearing capacity, her neglect in not calling the police immediately, her description of the driver, and the exact words she had told the police. Ruth wished she could protect the elderly lady from the merciless onslaught. Could the jurors see how the lawyer was taking an honest, hard-working grandmother and attempting to paint a picture of a conspiring, neglectful old lady? Ruth hoped so.

* * *

As she was eating lunch in the courthouse cafeteria, Ruth confided to a group of friends that she had always wanted to see court proceedings, "but not this way—not when I am so emotionally involved."

Surprise and wonder filled her eyes as she looked up from her sandwich. "It's amazing, but I don't feel bitterness toward Gary Newmen today," she reflected. "The Lord took it away, otherwise I'd be bitter. I'm hotheaded," she added with a short laugh.

Her eyes caught Andy's. A pang of sympathy shot through her heart. Today was his birthday. Only a few of their closest friends knew. And she could tell they were uncomfortble. She could almost read their thoughts: "How do you say 'Happy Birthday' to a father who has just testified at the trial of his daughter's murderer?" Indeed, *how would she?*

Later, stepping off the elevator, she glanced down the corridor at the jurors who appeared relaxed and smiling, finishing lunch or reading magazines in their appointed area. If only she could talk to the mothers among them. She'd beg them to see justice done. She'd plead with them

171

to find him guilty.

As she sank into her seat, she saw Gary being led into the courtroom once more. No, she didn't feel any bitterness toward him today. Yet he must be punished. She was certain of that. Even the Saviour will judge the wrongdoers who reject Him. Gary's crime would not go overlooked then; nor should it now.

At the sight of New Holland's Chief of Police walking to the stand she became aware that the afternoon session had begun. As he told about the ten-week search, her own recollections loomed as spectres, shadowing the clarity of his details. A sudden tiredness gripped her and she leaned against Andy's shoulder as she listened to the description of the watershed area where Evie was eventually found. Parts had been searched two or three times, but because of the density of the undergrowth they had not been able to cover every square inch. Conscious of Andy's hand holding hers, she gave it a squeeze that made him wince.

Now charts were being shown to the jury. She observed one juror fingering his mustache while another shifted his position for a better view through his dark-rimmed glasses. The balding, gray-haired man appeared engrossed in his study of a nearby diagram. Again, a silent plea flooded Ruth's mind. "Please, please, understand. And do what is right."

Allowing her eyes to rove around the room, she saw the defendant take a sip of water as he glanced at his attorneys. Resuming his now-familiar stare, he seemed to pay no attention to the jury or the police chief as the prosecutor continued his questioning.

At the sight of her son, Junior, walking to the witness

stand, Ruth sat up, tense and alert. The casual mannerisms of her tall, lanky son belied the emotional turmoil which Ruth knew lay within.

With only a hint of apprehension, he began to testify. "That afternoon, before we even knew Evie was missing, Newmen parked at the end of our driveway and walked across the lawn to where I was mowing. He asked me if I knew where Evie was. I told him, 'I think she's over cleaning your house.'

"Newmen answered, 'I don't know. I didn't stop in.' "

"And then before he drove away he asked me what time it was."

Junior's voice was hoarse as he continued to testify. He told of his unsuccessful search for Evie, revealing that during his first check of Newmen's house, he had seen three one dollar bills on the mantel. But when he had returned to search the house a second time there were *five* one dollar bills! Junior confirmed earlier testimony by Ruth that she had seen five dollars on the mantel, also.

Ruth noticed Gary shifting his position slightly. The frustration was almost more than she could bear: a mystery—and the answer to it sitting so close. And yet so far away.

The final evidence presented during this day in the courtroom struck Ruth with sickening force. A red quilted-type blanket containing lengths of rope, a soiled terry cloth object, and a red engineer's hanky had been found on October 10, the day after Evie's body had been discovered. As it was exhibited and discussed by Officer Hartman, Ruth noticed that the defendant closed his eyes for a brief second, then sat forward in his seat with apparent interest.

173

Tension threatened to overwhelm Ruth. The mental picture of Evie bound, gagged and wrapped in a blanket was more than she could bear. As an escape, she allowed trivia to momentarily occupy her mind. She deliberately studied the judge's sideburns, his wire-rimmed glasses, and the shiny silver water pitcher that seemed to reflect the scene and play back the reactions of the participants. Once, the judge leaned back, wiped his mouth, adjusted his glasses, and then, expressionless, continued to listen.

It wasn't long until the afternoon recess was called, and, quivering inside, Ruth stood up. She saw Gary Newmen stroll out of the room, his flowered shirt open at the neck. His hands were held in front of him, as if expecting handcuffs which were not forthcoming.

*   *   *

Three brief testimonies followed the afternoon recess, and then, finally, this day in the courtroom was over! But the memories of it clung to Ruth's mind like a spider spinning a web.

In their hotel room just before retiring, Andy opened his Bible and began to read, " 'No temptation has overtaken you but such as is common to man; and God is faithful, who will not allow you to be tempted beyond what you are able, but with the temptation will provide the way of escape also, that you may be able to endure it.' "[1]

Here was comfort for her distress and strength for her weakness. Her tense spirit was soothed. She relaxed. Sleep came as a welcome friend, temporarily releasing her from the pain and suffering which met her at the dawn of each new day.

174

MONDAY
MAY 4, 1981

Chapter Twenty

Monday—May 4, 1981

The green leather chairs had the appearance of silent props, waiting for the players to enter and continue the drama whose end was yet to be written. The events of the past weekend blurred and faded away as Ruth walked into the courtroom and the all-too-familiar scene.

Four days had passed since she had testified on the witness stand.

Relieved that her part in the trial was over, she took her seat in the front row of the spectators' section. The public defender had assumed an air of concentration as he bit his glasses and propped the arm of his blue striped jacket on the table in front of him. The court reporter's eyes bypassed the stack of papers and briefcases as he studied the spectators who were arriving in a steady stream. Ruth was glad to see many friends and relatives. Their presence and sympathy offered more support than they'd ever know.

It wasn't long until the defendant entered with a half smile as he recognized his sister and brother-in-law sitting on the back bench. The jurors followed, marching smartly to their places, giving the impression of being alert and ready to begin this day's decison-making.

At the familiar order, "All stand, please," Ruth saw the judge enter. The intonation continued, "God save the Commonwealth—"

"Oh, dear God," Ruth whispered, "assist and work mightily today!"

Her thoughts returned to the courtroom in time to hear, "You may be seated."

Looking older and pale, Ruth steeled herself as the day's proceedings began. Today she would keep the floodgate of emotion tightly closed against the outpouring of apprehension and dread. Nevertheless, the anxiety she felt at the mention of Evie's blue denim jeans threatened to penetrate her dammed-up emotions and send them tumbling over her self-imposed barrier. She trembled as she heard the description of the jeans which had been found inside out in twisted fashion under Evie's arms.

Grabbing Andy's hand for security, she noticed him swallow at the description of how the rope had been wrapped around Evie's wrists six times. Her chin quivered as she saw the photo of the sock which had been stuffed down Evie's throat. How could she endure the agony which was beginning to overwhelm her?

Then, large envelopes containing articles of Evie's clothing were offered into evidence. With blurred vision she saw the jurors watching intently as they were shown a photo of Evie's yellow and white shirt. Ruth could visualize it—cut and torn. Torn like a mother's heart. Cut by grief and pain.

Slowly the courtroom scene cleared before her eyes. Glancing at the defendant, she observed that he exhibited no outward emotion. He merely looked straight ahead while the bag which contained Evie's yellow panties was being identified. Did it mean nothing to him? *Oh God, doesn't he even care?*

Ruth saw Officer Hartman, attired in an unaccustomed gray suit, sitting with his hands together, lightly touching his chin. Ruth shuddered as she imagined the private scene he must be remembering.

As her mind returned to the proceedings she became aware that a state policeman was relating an unsolicited remark which had been made on the way to the Harrisburg State Hospital. Gary Newmen had said, "I didn't do it. If I did such a thing. . .how could I? She's just a young girl." Ruth had not heard this before!

Gary leaned over and whispered to his attorney who quickly entered into the proceedings. Had the defendant been advised of his rights as he was taken into custody? Had he signed papers?

Oh, yes, take care of the rights of the criminal! But where are the rights of the victim? Where were Evie's rights as she was being murdered? Ruth found herself staring unwaveringly at Gary. "Why don't *you* get up today and tell what you remember about the torn clothing in the bags, or how her hands came to be tied, or. . . ."

The courtroom scene swam before her eyes in a sea of frustration.

"Will Ruth Fisher return to the stand?"

The demanding monotone pierced through Ruth's trou-

179

bled thoughts like an arrow entering its unsuspecting prey. It couldn't be! Numbness overtook her. She hadn't expected to be called to the witness stand again! Shaking, she somehow managed to stand up and begin what seemed like an impossible walk to her sudden appointment.

Pursing her lips and fighting a feeling of weakness, she found herself facing the jurors once more—that sea of faces which she had analyzed and with which she had silently pleaded for three days. And then. . .there it was! Evie's sock dangled before her face! Instantly Ruth felt lightheaded; an involuntary sigh escaped from somewhere deep within her being.

The prosecutor, who had appeared to be sympathetic in the past, now seemed cruel in his flamboyant exposure of the tangible evidence. She heard herself explaining that this sock was one that her two daughters had worn interchangeably. But all she could see was the piece of cloth that had been stuffed down Evie's throat, cutting off her younger daughter's life breath forever. The navy and white striped sock was purplish-black from the collection of blood that had drained there as a result of her murderer's blows.

Ruth stiffened with apprehension as the manila envelopes were carried into her view. Somehow, with a strength that was not her own, she endured being shown photographs of their contents: Evie's bra, panties, top, and sneakers. Yes, yes, *yes*! They were *hers*! She fought back an almost uncontrollable urge to stand up, point to her former neighbor, and scream her accusation: "*He* did it! He cut them off her! Now make *him* tell exactly what he did to her. And *why*!"

Instead, she found herself faltering back down the aisle to her seat, crying silently as she passed the defendant, unable to bring herself even to look at him.

Refusing a requested recess, the judge insisted that the session continue with a report from the crime lab. Once again, the sock held the center of attention. Ruth was amazed at the endurance God gave her as she heard the grim story unfold.

Ruth's forebodings increased, however, as the proceedings focused on the description of the hair which had been taken from Gary's blanket. Three head hairs, five pubic hairs, and cat hair had been removed with the sweepings. When checked with a microscope, the head hairs were consistent with those taken from Evie's hairbrush!

The courtroom scene began to sway crazily before Ruth's eyes. A lump arose in her parched throat. She took a swallow of water from the cup she had set on the railing in front of her. The relief was only temporary.

Newmen's attorney pitched a question which he apparently hoped would strike out the effect of the morning's considerations: "Was the lab furnished with fingernail clippings of the defendant?"

Receiving a positive reply, he pursued, "What was the result of the tests?"

The witness from the crime lab intoned, "No blood, no flesh, normal debris."

His voice smacking of success, Newmen's counsel questioned further until he elicited the fact that no blood was found on the yellow and white blouse, underclothes or sneakers, either.

Seeing the point the defense attorney hoped to establish, Ruth wanted to protest in disbelief. No blood! That didn't

181

change the fact that her clothes had been cut off. That didn't change the fact that Evie was dead!

As if in a dream, Ruth heard the jurors being dismissed until 9:00 the following morning. Looking at her watch, she saw that it wasn't even lunchtime, yet they must wait another day for the tension to tighten—or uncoil. She knew her endurance had been stretched to its limit.

"But God is faithful, who will not suffer you to be tempted above that you are able."[1] The verse that Andy had asked her to read several nights before flashed through her mind.

She stood up. Once again, she placed her faith in God's promise. Once more she knew that she would have whatever strength she needed until this ordeal was over.

FRIDAY
JULY 31, 1981

Chapter Twenty-One

Friday—July 31, 1981

Ruth folded the dough toward her with her fingers, then pushed it away with the heel of her hand. Rotating it a quarter turn, she repeated the folding-pushing motion. As she added flour to the board, she remembered how much Evie had liked to knead dough, stopping only when it was smooth and satiny. Her little girl would place it carefully in a greased bowl, and, several times during the next hour and a half, she would gingerly lift one edge of the damp cloth, eager to watch her creation rise.

"May I punch it?" she'd plead after it had doubled in size. Her laughter would ring out as she jabbed the bloated dough, releasing the air bubbles.

Evie had laughed a lot.

But now it was July 31, 1981, and her daughter's laughter had been missing for a year. Ruth glanced at the kitchen clock. Shortly after noon today it would be one year since Evie had walked out of her mother's life—but not out of her heart. Evie would always have a special place in her heart.

The sudden bang of the screen door interrupted her painful memories. "Alma's here!" a voice sang out behind her back.

Ruth took a deep breath and turned to face her three-year-old son. His shining eyes and upturned face brought joy to her heart. She smiled through her tears. "Thank you, Lord, for all I have left," she murmured as she gave him an affectionate hug. "And thank you for friends who remember, and care."

*   *   *

Andy came home from the bakeshop in mid-afternoon, weary from the early hour he had risen. Ruth greeted him with what she hoped was a brave smile. Their embrace spoke of all the griefs and heartaches they had shared during the past year.

"Ummmm. Smells good! I love that aroma."

Ruth looked pleased as she removed the browned loaves from the oven and turned them out of the pans onto racks to cool.

"We'll be able to slice one of the loaves in just a little while for part of our lunch. I thought some apple butter on warm bread would make a good dessert."

As Ruth joined Andy at the table with her salad, he took her hand. "I've been thinking about all that God has been accomplishing in our lives. For one thing, we learned to go to the Word of God instead of sitting around, crying on each other's shoulders." He sat back a minute, reflecting some more before he added, "That really made a difference in our lives!"

Ruth's coffee cup clattered in her saucer as she spoke. "Yes, I'm sure God helped me through His Word during those days of the search. After I read of His miracle in taking the children of Israel across the Red Sea on dry ground I kept reminding Him of His mighty power."

Light shone in Andy's eyes as he continued, "And, Ruth, through our suffering other lives have been changed, too. God has touched hearts. He gave me the precious opportunity to lead Howard to Him, and we have received numerous phone calls from other people who have come to know the Lord Jesus personally because of what happened to Evie. They became aware of the need to be ready to give an account to God *now*. There may be no tomorrow."

The whistle of the local train as it rumbled down the nearby track was the only sound that could be heard for the next minute. Andy's sigh blended with the engine's mournful wail as he confided, "Ruth, when Newmen* was found guilty of first-degree murder I was glad to see justice being done! In fact, I hoped he would receive the death penalty instead of life imprisonment. I haven't always been consistent in my concern about his soul. But when I see things the way God sees them, I fear for his eternal destiny. I often pray that he will repent and accept Christ as his Saviour."

Ruth interrupted with a quiver in her voice, "Sometimes it's still hard for me to pray for his salvation. The fact that he has never talked and we don't really know why he killed Evie has made it easy for me to open the door to resentment. It began to take hold of me as soon as Evie

187

was missing, and that's when I began to pray that I wouldn't be enslaved by a bitter spirit toward him. But I can't say that it never comes up. It does. Especially when we go to the place in the mountains where Evie was found."

Andy twirled his coffee cup in his hand. "I understand, Ruth. Who would be harder to love than the person who killed your daughter? Yet, Jesus died for *him* just like He died for us. And God may be working in Newmen's heart. I hear he has contacted several preachers and expressed an interest in taking a Bible study correspondence course. We *must* continue to pray for him."

As Ruth listened she felt an intense gratitude for her husband rise within her. "I thank God for you daily, Andy." She squeezed his hands. "Your strong, consistent faith has been an example to me when I couldn't see even a glimmer of hope in my despair."

Avoiding his eyes, she confessed, "I often find it hardest to live for the Lord at home. I'm tempted to just 'be myself.' "

She continued with a short, hollow laugh. "I guess that really means that I let 'self' take charge. But, Andy, *your* faith in the Lord doesn't waver, even when we're alone here at home!"

Tears glistened in Andy's eyes. "Ruth, I praise God and give Him the credit for any faith I have. It isn't me, Andy Fisher, who is strong. It's my Lord who is strong *in* me. He has given me the firm conviction that He allowed all this to happen for a purpose."

Ruth could hear the pain in his voice as he slowly added, "*You* know that my faith wasn't always strong. Remember when we put the fleece out like Gideon and asked the Lord not to let it rain on Evie? We even specified that He keep the side of the road dry."

Running his fingers through his hair, he continued, "Then, the night it rained and we drove up Route 897 and saw the two-toned road, I got out and touched it, instead of believing that the lighter side was dry. I thought it *felt* damp. We even discussed the possibility that macadam had been laid on one side recently.

"But when you and Davy checked it out later on a clear day, you discovered that the road hadn't been patched! It was the same all the way across!

"*Now* we know that we were near Evie."

Choking on his words, Andy lamented, "We failed! We didn't see the answer! No, that isn't right, either. We saw it; we just didn't *believe* it!"

Placing her hand on his bowed head, Ruth tried to comfort her distraught husband. "Andy, don't feel so badly. We couldn't have saved Evie anyway."

Wiping her eyes, she added, "Of course, it would have avoided a lot of hard work. It was before the landfill search."

With more confidence, she declared, "Well, God remained faithful to us even if we lacked the faith to believe."

"Yes," Andy raised his head. "Maybe it was before His timing." But he wasn't able to conceal the doubt in his voice.

"Andy, we *are* learning to commit our lives to the Lord daily and then trust Him to guide us, no matter what happens. I've heard you say more than once that we ran to the Lord like a child runs to his father when he's hurt. I often think of that when Davy comes to you with one of

189

his problems. Sometimes they're real, and sometimes they're imaginary. But you listen to them all. And God listens to us."

"You're right, Ruth. We can always turn to the One who loved us so much that He gave His life for us. Sometimes I wonder why the great Creator would humble Himself and die in my place, for my sins, on a cross of agony and shame."

For a minute all was quiet. Only the distant barking of a dog could be heard. Then, picking up a knife, Andy began to slice one of the freshly baked loaves of bread. While spreading the mouth-watering chunk with apple butter, he mused, "I've seen God answering prayer in little things—and in big things—throughout this ordeal. And I'm sure He has answered in some ways that we won't be aware of this side of eternity."

Watching Andy as he hungrily devoured his bread, Ruth remembered her own encounter with the Lord. She decided that now was the time to tell her husband about it.

Taking a deep breath she began to share, "I'm thankful that during Evie's funeral I came to know Jesus, my Saviour, in a more real way than I ever had before." Her eyes fell on the loaf before them as she continued, "During the search I often doubted my own salvation. Now I know I'm saved and I'm experiencing the strength that He alone provides, especially during the darkest hours."

"Ruth, I've known."

Andy's eyes were tender. "I've seen the change in your life. I've seen His peace sustain you in the midst of our turmoil." He lowered his voice. "And I, too, have been comforted by your faith that kept shining through our midnight hour of trial and testing."

Ruth opened her mouth, but no words formed. Praise grew and filled her mind and heart.

Slowly she became aware of Andy studying the piece of bread in his hand. "This bread gives nourishment to our physical bodies, but God has also given all we've needed to strengthen us spiritually. He remained true to His promise to satisfy the poor with bread. He sustained us through His beloved Son, Jesus Christ, the Bread of Life. And, as our Saviour and Friend, He'll continue to provide for us now and in the coming days and years."

Hand in hand, with bowed heads, they thanked the One who had proven Himself so faithful on their behalf. They knew that they could commit their future to the faithful Guide who had walked with them in the past.

They had His own promise: "Be strong and courageous, do not be afraid or tremble at them, for the Lord your God is the one who goes with you. He will not fail you or forsake you."[1]

*The name of the man convicted of the murder of Evie Fisher has been changed to protect the family. The name used is fictitious and no reference to anyone living or dead is intended.

191

Author's Epilogue

Often one wonders what he or she would do if confronted by such a tragedy.

But from the moment Ruth looked into my eyes and asked, "What has he done with her?" a rush of sympathy spurred me to action. Something had to be done. *I* had to do something. But what? I floundered for an appropriate answer, but to no avail. A shared sigh, an exchanged glance, a sympathetic tear meant much. Just my being there seemed to bolster Ruth's spirits.

My husband and I shared daily visits with the Fishers, sometimes twice a day, but we were always careful not to stay too long. Sometimes we sat with them for fifteen minutes without saying a word. Our hearts suffered together. No words were needed. We did not force Scripture verses on them, nor did we always pray audibly.

Andy would sometimes vent his frustrations along with the latest news of the search. Often, in spite of the negative reports, he would pass Bibles to each of us and share from the Word that day's blessing which the Lord had given him. Before we went home, *we* were the ones who were encouraged!

Meanwhile, our five children were stricken with the implication of Evie's disappearance. At no time did they believe she had run away. They had known her. Especially Nancy, our daughter who was Evie's age. At first they were hesitant to go along and offer their sympathy to Evie's remaining sister and three brothers. They had never encountered such a situation and their first inclination was to "watch and pray" at a distance. After the initial shock, however, one by one they shyly accompanied us. It wasn't long before one or two asked to go along when we made our daily check.

Our family's lifestyle changed overnight. We rescheduled our normal routine so we could spend time with the Fishers. We spent more time in prayer and in contacting others, requesting prayer concerning the latest developments. We assisted in composing prayer letters that were sent to churches and other Christian organizations across the country. And we found that our minds were never free from concern nor our hearts from sharing the burden. Restless nights and troubled days took their toll on our strength. Our lives were now entwined with the Fishers'.

Fear for our own children began to grip us. We live in a rural area dotted with peaceful farms and friendly neighbors. Our two teenage girls loved to run along the country roads. There had always been a sense of safety, for "nothing ever happens to anyone here." Now we forbade them to leave our property unless an adult accompanied them.

Hope met each new day. Maybe *today* the searchers would find her! Each day ended in frustration. New leads had been followed, but with no success.

Slowly our faith increased as we learned to rely on God alone to perform a miracle and lead the searchers to Evie. God seemed to assure us that He *was* hearing our prayers and He *would* answer—in His time. Painfully, He taught us patience and the ability to rejoice in His faithfulness in spite of circumstances.

We found our outlook changing. Petty annoyances lost their importance. We laughed at our mistakes. We tolerated habits of family members which had previously disturbed us. After all, we were together. Our family circle was intact. And for that, we were grateful.

When Evie was finally found and the funeral plans were made, our children agreed to do what they felt was impossible: sing Evie's favorite song, "Oh, How I Love Jesus" and play "Victory in Jesus" on their brass instruments. I read a poem that had been sent to Andy and Ruth by a sympathizer who had composed it herself. The children and I leaned hard upon the Lord to control our emotions so we would be able to minister effectively.

Although I am a teacher in a Christian school, the principal graciously gave me permission to attend two days of the trial. Seeing Ruth's agony as she testified those two days was heart-rending. How helpless I felt! No matter what the outcome of the trial, Evie was gone. Ruth's loss was permanent and unjustified. I could only pray. And reach out with a touch.

It was sometime before the trial when I, with my husband's approval, offered to write the book that Andy desired would "minister to the needs of others so that Evie did not die in vain." Little did I know then how much that offer would affect my own family—and that in a sense we would all work on the project together. It was their understanding and encouragement that made the completion of such an undertaking possible.

At this writing, it has been four years since Evie's disappearance, and I have spent hundreds of hours sorting the material and rewriting the manuscript. Each of those hours represents time that my family allowed me to do what I knew to be God's will.

It is our desire that needy souls come to our Saviour and

receive eternal life; and that those who are suffering similar losses may find some word of encouragement and some source of help that will enable them to continue living their own lives with more strength and purpose than they believed was possible.

Fay L. Overly

Epilogue
by Andy Fisher

Perhaps the greatest sustaining force in my life since Evie's death is my belief that she did not die in vain. I believe with all my heart that her death and the long search were no surprise to God. He knew all the time where she was. But there was something He wanted to do through her death. There was a reason for it.

Even before Evie was missing, I felt that the most important aspects of a Christian's life are fellowship, worship, and praise on a regular basis. If we do these things, He *will* use us. We need a constant, day-by-day walk with Him. We need to trust Him. Since my personal time of trial, my spiritual life has deepened and I've drawn closer to the Lord. I try to surrender everything to Him on a daily basis.

I'm more convinced than ever that parents should take their children to church and read the Bible and pray with them. Children need to be encouraged in the ways of the Lord. During those weeks when Evie was missing we learned that sooner or later everyone needs a leaning post or crutch. We must have a place to go. We can't handle life by ourselves. We will go somewhere. If we don't turn to the Lord, we'll turn someplace else—maybe to alcohol or to drugs.

Some people say, "Why did this happen to you? You're such a good man." But I'm not such a good man. It's only by the grace of God that I'm saved.

There are two powers in the world: the power of God and the power of Satan. The man who killed my daughter listened to Satan. God is not a dictator. We're free moral agents and can choose to worship Him or allow Satan to deceive us.

I wouldn't trade the peace that God gives for anything in the world. Recently I was having devotions in the woods near our cabin when I experienced the same presence of the Lord that Ruth and I sensed after Evie was found. His presence is more wonderful than anything in the world. It passes all understanding. And to think that Evie is with the Lord and is experiencing it all the time!

We find that we're able to comfort others who are sorrowing in a more compassionate way since Evie's death. When an Amish lady was murdered in our town we were able to comfort her relatives by remembering our experience. We understood how the Bittermans felt when their son, Chet, was martyred as a missionary with Wycliffe in Colombia. We tried to follow the Overlys' example. When they came to see us, they didn't need to say anything. They were just there. Sometimes we prayed together and read Scripture. But often they just sat with us and ministered to us with their presence. That meant more to us than people who popped in, giving us pat Scriptural answers like they were handing out medicine for an instant cure.

Not that I don't love and respect the Bible. When Evie was missing I had the best counsel in the world in the holy Scriptures. I often went to the cellar alone. There I prayed and wept over the Word. Psalm 118 was one of my favorites and I read it over and over. Also Psalm 46 and Psalm 139. I bathed myself in the Psalms, almost forgetting there were other Scriptures! It was through the Word that the Holy Spirit gave me the grace to get through the time of trial.

Since the tragedy, our family is closer and has a new unity of spirit. We're more sensitive to each other. Ruth and I are more tolerant of each other. I recognize areas of strength in her I didn't see before. I've found that she was right in her judgment about many things concerning Evie and our experience.

We often look back and remember when Evie was with us. We wonder what if we'd done this or that. We've discussed how the crime could have been prevented. We thought we knew Newmen, but he deceived us. I guess we had relaxed our guard by feeling that something like that "can't happen here." We should have respected our first impulse, even if we didn't have any tangible facts to back it up. And I would advise young people to accept their parents' judgment even if they feel the parents are being too careful.

Everything in life is a learning experience, however. If we make something constructive out of events that come our way, we have grown.

Emotional Upheaval

If you are perplexed by varying emotions, do not feel alone. Upheaval can be expected during times of extreme trauma and grief. Just as Christ wept, showing His emotions at the tomb of Lazarus, your emotions must find their release. While emotions may differ with circumstances, they should be seen as a companion to grief. The following list of emotional releases are common.

1. Paralyzing fear as the possibility of a tragedy becomes apparent
2. Irrational actions and decisions
3. Shock that may trigger a physical reaction
4. Resentment and bitterness toward the cause of your grief
5. Impatience toward others whose outward calm is mistaken for indifference
6. Despair as the weight of the burden begins to be felt
7. Difficulty in praying, and the questioning of God's love and concern
8. Openly rebelling against what God has permitted to happen
9. Inner turmoil that refuses to be comforted
10. Emotional and physical exhaustion
11. Imaginations that cause the problem to appear even worse than it really is
12. Attachment of unrelated frustrations to the primary source of agitation
13. "Seesawing" emotions—surging hope to emptiness and despair
14. Hysteria at loss of hope
15. Temporarily desiring not to know the outcome
16. Blocking unbearable facts from your mind
17. Acting out of character
18. Taking "leaps of faith"
19. Questioning why God isn't (apparently) answering prayer

20. Mounting apprehension as time goes by without a solution
21. Inability to accept the truth
22. Cutting pain and empty hopelessness
23. Relief when the ordeal of waiting is over
24. Calmness stemming from God's grace and peace
25. Intermingled praise and anguish as memories flood your mind
26. Comfort from God Himself
27. Second-guessing yourself and torturous "What if?" questions
28. Anger toward the assailant
29. Hostility toward a godless world that breeds violence and crime
30. Detachment from reality
31. Mechanical acceptance of condolences
32. An empty void as the finality of your loved one's departure is indelibly imprinted on your heart
33. Living in the past
34. Desire for immediate revenge
35. Retreating into your own private world as an escape
36. Experiencing an infused strength that is not your own
37. Inability to dispel the remembered past that accompanies today's tasks
38. Deep gratitude for understanding friends, relatives, and "strangers" who help beyond their duty

Active Steps to Take During a Crisis

Perhaps as you are reading this you, or someone you

know, is experiencing a similar tragedy. You may feel helpless and wonder what you can do. The following steps of action, taken from our experience, may prove helpful to you.

1. Ask for, and accept, the assistance of friends, acquaintances and organizations who are less emotionally involved and better equipped to make rational judgments.

2. Go to the Scripture for comfort and strength in spite of your feelings.

3. Look to God for the solution to the problem and give Him the glory in advance for what He is going to do.

4. Request prayer. Make your situation known.

5. Maintain as normal a family routine as possible.

6. Cooperate with the investigation. Pray for the police and investigators. Actively support them.

7. Vent your emotions to your husband or wife or a close friend. Air your frustrations with them.

8. Share the gospel wherever possible through your life and testimony.

9. Keep a record of the search. Begin an album of newspaper clippings.

10. Keep busy. Become involved with creative activities while you wait.

11. Think of ways to memorialize your lost loved one that will benefit others such as buying time on a radio station for Scripture reading, renting an advertising space in a public place for a Scripture verse, purchasing hymn books for your church in the name of your loved one, furnishing a room in your local hospital, assisting in a

project at your Christian school, etc.

12. List what you have learned from the suffering you endured.

13. List ways in which other people have been ministered to through this tragedy.

14. Ask God to replace your bitterness and resentment with His love.

15. Become involved with the living. Comfort other family members, even while you feel the need for support.

Inner Determinations

Perhaps not seen outwardly, but just as important, are inner determinations that will strengthen you and allow you to be a positive influence during a chaotic time.

Determine not to become part of the problem—but part of the solution. Face the situation and do what you have to do. Depend on God for the necessary strength.

Determine to face the truth and live with reality, unpleasant as it may be at the time.

Determine to allow God to work in your heart and life through these adverse circumstances. Learn how older or more mature Christians have handled similar situations.

Determine not to give up! Never lose hope.

Determine to accept the outcome, whatever it may be.

Determine not to make unreasonable demands on yourself or others. Allow for errors in judgment and varying opinions.

Determine to carry on in the strength of the Lord for the

sake of other family members.

Determine to look to the future with the renewed hope and courage that is found by committing it to God.

For further information, encouragement or to share experiences, please feel free to contact:

Andrew and Ruth Fisher
c/o Accent Books
P.O. Box 15337
Denver, Colorado 80215

Resources

The following list of resources and counselors should not be construed as an endorsement by the publisher or the author. There are numerous highly qualified counseling centers and counselors available throughout the country. These suggestions are given as a starting point to find the comfort and professional guidance sometimes necessary during times of intense emotional turmoil.

EAST

Adam Walsh Child Resource Center
1876 North University Drive
Fort Lauderdale, Florida 33322
(305) 475-4622

Biblical Counseling Foundation
615 South Wakefield Street
Arlington, Virginia 22204
(703) 243-8444
* Certified by the National Association of Nouthetic Counselors

Christian Counseling and Educational Foundation
1790 East Willow Grove Avenue
Laverock, Pennsylvania 19118
(215) 884-7676
* Certified by the National Association of Nouthetic Counselors

Christian Counseling Institute
National Resource Center Headquarters
P.O. Box 899
Lancaster, Pennsylvania 17603
(717) 394-8871

* Christian Counseling Institute is a resource center to encourage Biblical counseling in the local church. They provide training materials and assistance for churches and laymen to develop local church counseling ministries. They also provide Biblical counseling on death, dying, grief and bereavement.

Forestdale Counseling Ministry
11 Tabor Road, Box 289
Forestdale, Massachusetts 02644
(617) 477-1409
* Certified by the National Association of Nouthetic Counselors

Counseling Center
Grace Fellowship International—Atlanta
1501 Johnson Ferry Road
Suite 135
Marietta, Georgia 30062
(404) 973-5828

Counseling Center
Grace Fellowship International—Clearwater
1100 Cleveland Street
Suite 206
Clearwater, Florida 33515
(813) 442-1355

Granada Pastoral Counseling Center
950 University Drive
Coral Gables, Florida 33134
(305) 444-4622
* Certified by the National Association of Nouthetic Counselors

Lake Avenue Counseling Ministry
Box 285 West Sand Lake
West Sand Lake, New York 12109
(518) 674-2958
* Certified by the National Association of Nouthetic Counselors

Counseling Center
Liberty Baptist College
Thomas Road Baptist Church

P.O. Box 20000
Lynchburg, Virginia 24507
(804) 239-0405

Middle Georgia Pastoral Counseling Center
682 Mulberry Street
Macon, Georgia 31201
(912) 746-3223
* Certified by the National Association of Nouthetic Counselors

National Association of Nouthetic Counselors
1516 Ancona Avenue
Coral Gables, Florida 33146
(305) 667-4850
* The National Association of Nouthetic Counselors monitors and
certifies Biblical counseling centers across the United States. This
office serves as a national referral center for all programs that have
met their rigorous standards. Nouthetic counseling is a Scripturally
based approach that challenges individuals to examine themselves
and their needs according to standards and methods set forth in the
Bible.

The National Center for Missing and Exploited Children
1835 K Street, N.W.
Suite 700
Washington, D.C. 20006
(202) 634-9821 (general information and requests for assistance)
(800) 843-5678 (citings only)
* The National Center keeps up-to-date lists of programs throughout
the United States. Only those programs with a paid staff and officers
are included.

CENTRAL

Faith Baptist Counseling Ministries
2925 South 18th Street
Lafayette, Indiana 47905
(317) 474-9806
* Certified by the National Association of Nouthetic Counselors

Counseling Center
Grace Fellowship International—Denver
1455 Ammons Street
Denver, Colorado 80215
(303) 232-8870

Counseling Center
Grace Fellowship International—Indianapolis
888 Southview Road
Indianapolis, Indiana 46227
(317) 787-5662

Counseling Center
Grace Fellowship International—Springfield
1722 West Glenstone Square
Suite 201
Springfield, Missouri 65804

Dr. Larry Crabb
Chairman, Department of Biblical Counseling
Grace Theological Seminary
Winona Lake, Indiana 46590
(219) 269-6741
* The Grace Theological Seminary Counseling Center offers individual
  counseling and referrals to private counselors trained in Biblical
  intervention.

Henry Kemp Center for Study of Child Abuse
International Headquarters
1205 Oneida Street
Denver, Colorado 80220
(303) 321-3963
* The Henry Kemp Center works primarily with the families of children
  who are victims of physical, sexual and emotional assault. They also
  advise the courts on appropriate prosecution of such cases.

Missing Children Network
2211 South Dixie Drive
Dayton, Ohio 45409
(800) 235-3535
* The Missing Children Network is a nationally syndicated news/infor-

mation report. The network assists parents by securing television air time on news programs throughout the country at no cost to the parents. Launched in April 1984, the non-profit subscribing organizations affiliated with the Missing Children Network have reported a 32% success rate at this printing.

WEST

Christian Counseling and Educational Foundation
3495 College Avenue
San Diego, California 92115
(619) 582-5554

Christian Counseling and Educational Foundation
    (West Branch)
2734 Keen Drive
San Diego, California 92139
(619) 475-4635
* Certified by the National Association of Nouthetic Counselors

Family Life Seminars
Dr. Tim LaHaye
Counseling Department
P.O. Box 16000
San Diego, California 92116
(619) 440-0227

Dr. Clyde Narramore
Psychology for Living
Box 5000
Rosemead, California 91770-0950
(818) 288-7000 (Referral Department)

Rosemead Counseling Services
Rosemead School of Psychology
Biola University
Two Locations:

1409 North Walnut Grove	13800 Biola Avenue
Rosemead, California 91770	La Mirada, California 90639
(818) 288-7150	(213) 946-1761

Scripture Footnotes

Chapter 3
1. Exodus 14:29, NIV

Chapter 4
1. Acts 2:21, KJV
2. John 6:35, NASB

Chapter 5
1. Isaiah 40:29-31, NASB

Chapter 6
1. NASB

Chapter 8
1. Ephesians 6:11, NASB
2. Ephesians 6:12, NASB
3. Ephesians 6:12, NASB

Chapter 10
1. Psalm 119:133, NASB
2. NASB
3. Luke 8

Chapter 11
1. Psalm 37:1, NASB

Chapter 12
1. See Ephesians 6:4.

Chapter 14
1. Philippians 1:12, NASB
2. Philippians 1:29, NASB

Chapter 15
1. John 3:36, KJV
2. Romans 3:23, KJV
3. Ephesians 2:8-9, KJV
4. John 14:6, KJV
5. NASB

Chapter 16
1. Psalm 62:8, NASB
2. Psalm 56:3-4, NASB
3. Psalm 72:12, NASB

Chapter 17
1. NASB
2. Proverbs 11:5b, NASB
3. Proverbs 11:21, NASB
4. I Peter 4:19, NASB
5. Psalm 5:11, NASB

Chapter 18
1. Romans 12:19, NASB
2. I Corinthians 4:5, NASB

Chapter 19
1. I Corinthians 10:13, NASB

Chapter 20
1. I Corinthians 10:13, NASB

Chapter 21
1. Deuteronomy 31:6